Restoring Trust

The Handbook of Integral Management

L. David Montague

ISBN 9798667728917
Copyright 2002

ACKNOWLEDGEMENTS

The author wishes to express his appreciation to Phyllis B. Melnick for her dedicated assistance in editing, critiquing and proof reading the text of 'Restoring Trust'.

He also owes a debt of gratitude to his late son Mark David Montague for his immense help in final editing and formatting the figures and text for the book for its initial electronic version and the paperback version. He believed in and lived his life consistent with the precepts of the book and 'Restoring Trust' is dedicated to his memory.

FOREWORD

First written two **years** before the "dot com" implosion and the Enron scandal, *Restoring Trust* foresaw today's crisis in American business and government. Sound management practices have all but been eclipsed by the recent and seemingly endless revelations of fraud and excess at the highest level, often aided and abetted by the financial community. The recent carnage in the 2007-2008 financial meltdown is the product of management practices perverted by personal greed, based neither on good corporate governance or good corporate citizenship. The betrayal of public trust has destroyed confidence in Corporate America, its so-called independent analysts, and its regulators.

The excesses and collapse of the 'dot com' driven "new economy" at the turn of the millennium, and recent revelations of corporate fraud by senior management of Enron, Anderson and others did not occur over-night. They evolved during the last 20 years, which saw the junk bond leveraged buy outs of the 80's, and the corporate merger mania of the 90's fueled by over-inflated paper value hyped by Wall Street. These were the harbingers of what was to come.

The Author
Dave Montague is a retired Division President of a major aerospace corporation and a Vice President of the parent Corporation.

A 1956 engineering graduate of Cornell University, Dave began as a first level design engineer in a new division of Lockheed, the company where he was to build his professional career. He progressed through various technical and management assignments and was selected to lead the definition and implementation of a multi-billion dollar development and initial production program for the Navy Trident I submarine based strategic missile system. He went on to become a Vice President over several defense programs, where he directed Lockheed's efforts that accomplished the first "hit to kill" interception and destruction of an Intercontinental Ballistic Missile reentry vehicle high above the atmosphere in 1984. Dave was elected an Officer of Lockheed Corporation in

1989. He ran a 1.6 billion dollar enterprise of more than 6,000 engineering and manufacturing professionals engaged in development, production and support for the Fleet Ballistic Missile programs, Defensive Missile Systems -- most notably the Theater High Altitude Area Defense System, Lockheed's low-cost space launch vehicle program, marine systems programs, and several smart weapons programs before retiring in early 1996,

Mr. Montague, is a leader in project and systems management, nationally recognized for his expertise in strategic and tactical strike and defensive weapon systems design, management and policy. He is a fellow of the American Institute of Aeronautics and Astronautics. In 1991 he was elected a member of the National Academy of Engineering.

He has served as an advisor to the Department of Defense on strategic weapons and space applications, including several Defense Science Board task forces. He also has served on studies for the U.S. Army in ballistic missile defense and for the National Research Council Naval Studies Board. He participated in studies for the Georgetown Center for Strategic and International Studies examining strategic force posture and policy.

Since retiring, Mr. Montague has consulted for various companies and government agencies on systems engineering and project management issues and has authored numerous papers on national defense policy issues and management topics in conjunction with his service on defense policy studies.

The Book
In *Restoring Trust*, Mr. Montague focuses on the effective management of enterprises and projects of all shapes and sizes in today's rapidly changing environment. Building on 40 years of high integrity management success, he sets the stage, examining many management issues and pitfalls, the forces at work and their ramifications over the last 20 years.

Restoring Trust builds a foundation of key principles, from the perspective of all the stakeholders in an enterprise of any size, offering specific remedies and management methods proven successful in establishing and maintaining credibility at all levels in the business environment. He calls this approach to enterprise and project leadership "Integral Management".

The book offers several unique features:

- Insight into the real world roles and relationships of successful project and enterprise management teams
- A road map to recognize and navigate through pitfalls of project and organization management
- A handbook "hands on" approach to achieving an environment of integrity and trust in all facets of enterprise activity and management.
- Comprehensive presentation of proven methods with examples of their use in successful enterprises
- Examination of model organizational alternatives and behavior that can help or hinder success.

Table of Contents

Prologue

This book is written in the belief that management dedicated to the principles of integrity, equity and uncompromising honesty is the foundation upon which successful enduring companies flourish. In today's environment of mergers and consolidations, these principles have been pushed aside and forgotten, trampled by the stampede to this year's bottom line, and a surfeit of management fads.

Disturbing Signs in American Business

Did you ever ask yourself why we are here? I mean, why do we exist? At the end of our time, when we take stock, what would we like to feel we accomplished in life? It has always been my simple view that each of us was put on this earth to leave things better than we found them.

For more than 20 years, the business schools of this country have produced many graduates that entered the investment community and management consulting industry well grounded in leveraged buy-outs, junk bonds, arbitrage, and corporate strategic positioning, but with little knowledge about the arts of effective management. The measure of success has been near term rate of return. Those years seem to have spawned a hard-edged management philosophy which values ruthless style, greed, and predatory behavior over sound management practices.

One product of these years was the binge of leveraged buyouts that occurred in the 1980's. There is little doubt that many American companies grew complacent and slow to adapt
to changes in the competitive environment and were in serious need of overhaul. It is also true that many well run companies

fell victim to the frenzy of leveraged acquisitions financed by junk bonds and the subsequent disassembly of those businesses. This predatory behavior fueled what some say was the largest loss of US industrial productivity since the end of World War 2.[1]

A second product of this environment has been the rise in management fads based on unproven theories, and theoretical but often bogus measures of effectiveness. What is most disconcerting is the readiness of senior corporate management to act with herd mentality in response to these fads. Spurred on by the near term bottom line, increased global competition and loss of market share, many senior executives have embraced the faddish teachings of the newest management gurus following each other down what seems a self-destructive path. A 1997 National Research Council Study[2] concluded that many of these "innovations" have been embraced by both industry and government with inadequate evaluation or understanding, and dubious benefit.

As we entered the 21st century, we have the age of mega-merger mania and so-called financial reengineering of enterprises. This has been one of the all-time great fads of modern business, encouraged by Wall Street. It has provided a veritable feeding frenzy for management consulting firms. Freshly minted MBA's armed with the latest theories, hired as "facilitators" are dispatched to help "reengineer" your new merged company. In the short term, this strategy can result in the perception of increased productivity by acquiring sales base by merger while eliminating jobs (euphemistically referred to as

---

[1] Attributed to Akio Morita, former Sony CEO

[2] *Enhancing Organizational Performance*   National Academy Press Publication,1997 Daniel Druckman, Jerome Singer, and Harold Van Cott, Editors

"right sizing") through consolidation. The long term is something else again. These decisions are made by people who are rewarded for this near-term performance by near term stock appreciation, but who will not be around when the corpus has bled dry.

It has been observed over the last 25 years that by any key measure, more than two thirds of all mergers fail.[3] Some fail to deliver the benefits envisioned, and some just fail. There is precious little new evidence to refute that assessment. The primary beneficiaries of a merger are those who put it together. With the exception of the financial investment community and a few key executives who profit from the initial spurt in stock value, who are the beneficiaries of the mega-mergers and consolidations that have become the darlings of the Street? Have customers benefited? Has middle management? Has the work force?

In the post-merger consolidation process, faddy noun-verb euphemisms have entered the vocabulary. "reengineering" of the enterprise, "right sizing", and "outsourcing". A current favorite is the practice of hiring long-term part time employees to avoid the obligations and cost of benefits. In all of these new "management" techniques, the work force bears the pain of the cost savings, with infrastructure cuts that ignore the long-term health of the enterprise. They all seem to illustrate a lack of management integrity and a lack of respect for employees.

Taking Stock
Near-term bottom line performance and steady growth is certainly important, but the long-term health of a corporation

---

[3] *Managing the Merger* Philip H. Mirvis and Mitchell Lee Marks. Prentis Hall 1992

depends on a balance between the short-term performance and long term growth. The financial investment community's enormous influence with its natural focus on near term performance ensures publicly held corporate management's financially incented homage to this focus. The result is distortion of good management practice, short term profit achieved by sapping the future life of the enterprise, destroying employee loyalty, productivity and corporate capability. Can any of these results be viewed as leaving things better than we found them?

Striking a Proper Balance

The thrust of this book is that management should be a win-win undertaking that requires the balancing of short and long-term objectives with high integrity.

I call this philosophy *integral management.* Integral Management suggests considering all the parts and interactions of the management job with an emphasis on mutual respect. The principles of this approach are based on management experience of 40 years of success during good times and bad. Its power is in its simplicity. But, like freedom, sustaining it requires vigilance.

Good management requires understanding the underlying forces that affect the enterprise. Too many managers today are too busy creating perception about the future, rather than assuring that future. Instead of understanding the underlying forces that are affecting the enterprise, we hear the words "vision" and "best practices" overused, while early tactical decisions based on real data are avoided. The result is that actions when finally taken are based on crisis control. These actions include saddling the future of the Enterprise with the costs of early out programs.

I have had the privilege of working, growing, and leading in a work environment that was the nexus of a high integrity company and high integrity customer relationships for all those years. Growing up with them as they evolved, learning and experiencing as they matured, I was able to witness and participate in their effectiveness first hand. I saw the successes and saw where failures occurred. I watched and dealt with other enterprises, both commercial and government where these qualities were not valued and saw how they performed. Each of the six or so leaders of this very successful enterprise, one of which I was privileged to be, added, updated and refined the ideas within the enduring framework. One thing I know for certain. They work! The proof is a 40 year record of on time performance exceeding requirements with a cumulative cost variance of less than 2 percent. When a company or agency truly operates in accordance with these qualities, it will consistently outperform others in virtually every way, including the bottom line.

The context of this book lies primarily in the experiences of the successful management of large technically challenging programs for the US Government. They were programs of national priority. They required substantial engineering and analytical efforts and invention on the fly, as well as solving unknown problems as they were discovered. As such, the customer and contractor teams bore an onus of public trust that was not taken lightly and pervaded every part of the activity. In today's environment the reader would be justified in being skeptical of that statement, and that is precisely the point of this book.

Virtually all of the principles espoused here apply to any business activity large or small. These principles are not revolutionary. They have evolved to meet new challenges and I have watched with awe as they fueled success. I have tried to update and capture these ideas on paper as we imbedded the philosophy in a totally new environment experiencing dramatic changes.

Scope of the book

This book examines most aspects of management, from the leadership of small groups, project management, functional management, to the general management of large enterprises. It is a book about the principles and disciplines of integral management, rather than particular tools of the management trade. There are many excellent books that address those aspects in detail. It is my hope that this book will show the need for these tools and spark interest in seeking out these sources.

While I hope this book is of value to anyone in business leadership, I have aimed it at those who are entering or in positions of project leadership.
I did so, for two reasons. First, the complexities of today's products, be they coffee pots, world wide web exploitation products, or interplanetary probes, are driven by engineering, and require effective project leadership. Second, projects are the venue where all the resources of an enterprise must be effectively marshaled to achieve the project goals. Those decisions can make or break a company or a project. Engineering managers should understand these principles as well as the general management.

Anyone looking for the magic shortcut to management miracles or the Rosetta Stone for instant success need read no further. They aren't to be found here. Good management is hard work and demands common sense, integrity, and an inquiring mind.

While grounded in experience in managing large complex projects that involved extensive development and engineering as well as production, this book can be a handbook for all forms of enterprises and new managers who want to create an environment of high integrity and trust in their business. It is my belief that these ideas will help them become effective leaders in their enterprise. From leading people, contract management, managing suppliers, managing resources and assets to organizing an en-terprise-- all of these are discussed in the context of uncompromising integrity, and its profound effect on building trust and high performance organizations.

Restoring Trust is dedicated to all of those who taught me these principles and to a future based on substance, not just form, and to actions that are congruent with words.

Chapter 1 Thesis

1.0 The Implications of Current Trends

As the mergers and consolidations of the 1990's mature, several trends are emerging. First, evidence shows that the current hard-edged approach to management has eroded trust between enterprise management and the work force, and after the apparent initial productivity increase due to layoffs and consolidation, a major loss in productivity has occurred. Why? Because distrust is a debilitating and contagious disease.

Second, this loss of productivity, and the accompanying loss of the recipe for success, has created distrust by customers as projected benefits of the merger fail to materialize and commitments fail to be met. In many cases, the impact of mergers has not only been below expectations, but negative. This is particularly evident in the aerospace, banking, energy, transportation, and public utilities sectors.

I believe a different approach is imperative. All managers at all levels of any enterprise have a fundamental responsibility to serve the interests of *all* the stakeholders of that enterprise with the highest integrity. This means living up to societal as well as financial measures of integrity. While easy to say, this is not an easy charge. For as we will see later, the higher the level of management, the more pressures there are to serve a limited segment of the stakeholders.

1.1 The Fragility of Trust

A business enterprise is a society within society. In any significantly sized enterprise, as in society, there are all kinds of people with different stakes, and with a diverse range of philosophies that govern their interactions with others. There are collaborative participants and those who lean toward advancing themselves at the expense of others, those with the courage of their convictions and those with none, those who value honesty and those who don't. The environment fostered within this microcosm of society determines in large part what that enterprise becomes.

No matter what it writes or says, *management demonstrates its true intent by what behavior is rewarded and tolerated.*
If collaboration and teamwork yielding good performance are rewarded and encouraged, they will grow. If self-serving advancement at the expense of others is not discouraged, it will prevail. If form is rewarded over substance, it will prevail. Far too often, driven by the need to seem effective, managers of enterprises big and small opt for form over substance. Disintegration of trust quickly follows.

When future outcome has at least the same present value as current perception, integrity will flourish. The converse is also true.

Think about those words and what they mean. It is what this book is about.

The American Heritage Dictionary defines **Integrity** as—the state of being unimpaired; soundness; honesty; completeness
Integral-- necessary to the whole; complete;
integrate -- to make into a whole by bringing together all parts; to unify; to unite; to make complete.
Integral! integrate! Integrity! What perfect words to describe the duty of management!

Integrity is largely about mutual respect. Most people like to work in an environment where they know what is expected and what to expect of their leaders and coworkers. They will take more initiative, and it has been demonstrated again and again that they will outperform other groups by far. What is it that makes this happen? It is mutual respect, pride....and trust.

Restoring Trust is about "Integral Management". That is bringing all the elements of managing together and performing them with uncompromising integrity.

1.2 The Challenge of Integral Management

Trust can only occur when integrity exists in all parts of your endeavor. There is no way that integrity applies or exists only in most actions or at certain times. The smallest lapse undermines trust. Failure to imbed integrity in some part of your business or your procedures can discourage people in other parts from believing you mean it. It is as if you were trying to weave a tapestry with one or more thread colors missing. Not only is the pattern incomplete, the fabric is weakened as well. We will see some examples of this pitfall later in this book.

1.3 Recognizing the Stakeholders

Management is about the relationships among people-- more specifically the stakeholders of the enterprise-- *all* of them. Typically, these include financial investors, executive management, customers, middle managers, long-term employees, short-term employees and suppliers. In the case of a government enterprise, the investors are the taxpayers and their representatives.

There are both long- and short-term stakeholders in this group. The concept of integral management recognizes that *all* the stakeholders are important to a successful, enduring enterprise, and strives to balance the interests of each to achieve cosistent and lasting success as measured by all the stakeholders. *Restor-*

ing Trust describes a style and set of relationships that recognizes all of these realities, while nurturing behavior proven to yield success at all levels of an enterprise, through good times and bad.

1.4 Adversity: The True Test of Management Integrity

Almost anyone armed with the bare essentials can manage an enterprise when times are good and the waters are smooth.

In writing this book, I became intrigued with the similarities between a convoy of ships and a business enterprise. In calm waters, with no enemy threat, the flagship's job is straightforward: set a course to the destination and tell the other ships how to position themselves and the planned rate of advance. Operations are routine and repetitive, and little guidance or integration is needed.

It is when the waters get rough and roiled that managers get tested. When stormy conditions blow the ships off course, the best course of action is uncertain. The entire convoy's future hangs on decisions made under stress. It is then that integrity and trust get tested as well. What counts at that time is the master mariner whose instincts, based on experience, can be trusted. If instead, feather merchants rule the quarterdeck, the fate of the Spanish Armada lurks near.

So it is with enterprise management. The principles presented in this book provide an **environment** where the entire management team can function and make needed decisions at their level with confidence about how the rest of the enterprise will respond. Consistent high-integrity behavior in no way suggests unbridled trust or naivety about dishonest or "unenlightened" behavior by others. Quite the contrary: people of integrity believe in defining the terms of a transaction fully to communicate expectations and avoid surprises. Business-like relationships cannot depend or survive on trust alone. Trust must be earned on a continuing basis. This issue is discussed at some length in later chapters of this book, along with related topics such as effective contracts and ethics.

1.5 Integrity in All Relationships

To set the stage, I would like to define eight key elements of integrity, shown in Figure 1-1, that underpin the relationships important to the success of a project, and to most other relationships as well. Introducing them here in the context of project management helps us begin "peeling the onion" of integral management and to add substance to an otherwise abstract concept.

An enterprise is only as good as its people, at all levels, and their motivation. Similarly, the most important ingredients in a project's success or failure are people, and how they interact to plan and execute the project. It follows then, that leadership must assure a healthy environment where trust and mutual cooperation can be taken for granted -- in other words, an environment of mutual respect.

The fundamental precept in a high-integrity work environment is the golden rule. How would you like to be treated if you were in someone else's shoes? Doesn't it make sense to treat others that way? The phrase "the ends justify the means" while generally condemned, is too often followed. It has no place in a high-integrity operation. While results are the measure of performance, success achieved at the expense of integrity and trust is likely to be short-lived.

WHAT'S IMPORTANT	KEY ISSUE
• PEOPLE • PROJECT SUCCESS • PERFORMANCE	• MAKE IT HAPPEN OR NOT • FIRST AND FOREMOST • RESULTS AND MEANS COUNT • IT'S ABOUT PEOPLE
• INTEGRITY	• INITIATIVE • PLANNING • COMMITMENT • OWNERSHIP • COMMUNICATION • HONESTY • TEAMWORK • RECOGNITION

Table1-1 Elements of Project Integrity

The eight elements of integrity shown in Table 1-1 are familiar terms, but I want to say a few words about what they mean to me in the context of all levels of enterprise management:

Initiative - This simply means not waiting to be told what to do. If you see something that needs doing, be willing to do it. Cover the under-laps.

Planning - There can be no integrity without a plan. It provides a solid basis on which to make commitments. If you don't have a plan, how do you know when you are falling short of requirements and need corrective action?

Commitment and ownership - Together, these mean taking personal responsibility, and the key to that is empowering the employees with the authority to get the job done. The other side of the coin is accountability for the results.

Honesty - If there is to be any confidence in the outcome of a plan, there must be trust among those working it. This means being honest about what can be achieved, and promptly making those who need to know aware of any problems that affect the outcome. If the project manager isn't honest with the team, the team is not likely to be honest with the project manager

Teamwork - True teamwork exists when people on a team ask each other "What is your objective, and how can I help you meet your objective while meeting my own?"

Communication - Expectations must be communicated clearly and mutually agreed to. The communication channels must remain open so that if there are problems in fulfilling a plan, they can be aired and dealt with.
The means of communicating in a large project or organization is crucial to its effectiveness and deserves a chapter of its own. Suffice it to say here that technological advances in communication media have both great benefits and serious shortcomings that can give the illusion of communication while failing miserably.

Recognition – The last element of integrity in this context is the fair and appropriate recognition for valuable contributions by individuals and team efforts. Acknowledgement of outstanding work is an effective way of communicating what is valued and appreciated in the project or enterprise and is often as important as money. In my experience, enterprises or projects where these eight elements are ingrained achieve high levels of performance. On the other hand, large cost overruns, missed schedules, and other troubles are the norm when they are missing. In later chapters, we will discuss these characteristics in more detail.

These tenets of integrity suggest the idea of contracts; contracts between individuals who depend on one another for commitments, and the meeting of those commitments; contracts between individuals and their supervisors on expectations and goals, as well as contracts between sellers and buyers. Indeed, contracts, whether formal or informal, are a key part of the fabric of integral management and will be a recurring theme in this book

Having established some definitions of the framework for integral management, we will turn now, in Chapter 2, to some fundamental management issues relating to the roles and division of management responsibilities in the evolution of an enterprise.

Subsequent chapters will examine the division of management in more detail with its effects on organization, and the management disciplines of the organizations that make up and guide the enterprise within which projects and products are created.

Chapter 2 Senior Management Roles

2.0 Introduction

This chapter will examine Enterprise management, its role, and some of the forces that influence upon those who undertake the job. Hereafter in the book I will use 'Enterprise' with a capital E to refer to the whole company, division, or entity to be managed, and will refer to the people who run that Enterprise as top or upper management. An analogy used earlier would be that the Enterprise is a convoy of ships. I will use 'enterprise' with a small e to refer to organizations analogous to the individual ships in the convoy, or the division of effort within the Enterprise

2.1 Some Observations about Enterprise Management

Successful Enterprises usually start out as enterprises – small, close-coupled, informal teams working on a single product or project. They are like a single ship. The individuals are all together within shouting distance of each other with more work to do than people to do it. If they are successful, the 'enterprise' grows into an 'Enterprise'. More people are hired to do the work, more products are launched and operations become more complex. Suddenly, new government regulations become applicable. Things that no one needed to worry about before take on new significance. The new people don't have the same shared vision of how things are to be done, or of the objectives of the Enterprise. Communication becomes a problem; hiring and policies and payroll taxes become more than time shared tasks. Things begin to get overlooked and sometimes get out of control without more formal arrangements. Individuals must become more focused on specialties and less Jacks of all trades. This division of labor becomes more important as the Enterprise grows as does the division of management responsibility. The ship becomes a group of ships trying to sail in convoy.

In this transition from a small number of people with a clear vision and knowledge of each other to a larger disparate group with longer lines of communications and legitimate conflicts in objectives, more formal checks and balances are needed to assure that the high integrity environment is not degraded.

2.2 Top Management's Real Job

What is the fundamental job of top management in an Enterprise? Facing *inward,* it is to guide the Enterprise in the conduct of its business, with the key word being "guide*."* It is to set standards and expectations. It is *not* to steer every ship in the convoy. That, along with all other activity required to maintain an individual ship in its proper position in the convoy, is the responsibility of the captain and crew of that ship.

Facing *outward,* the top management job is to represent the Enterprise to the outside world and look ahead to estimate how the outside world will perceive and influence the Enterprise. Most of the Enterprise is properly focused on the present and near future in the execution of its mission. Divining the longer-term future, and deciding how it will affect the Enterprise and its mission, is a hard job. So upper management shouldn't spend a lot of time steering even the lead ship in the convoy; if they're unwilling to delegate ship operations and face the more daunting task of guiding the convoy, they need reassignment.

Guiding the convoy means looking ahead, deciding on the best course, to take advantage of opportunities and avoid threats to the success of the convoy's mission. It also means thinking of tactics for seizing opportunities when they appear, and defending the convoy against those threats that cannot be avoided. But *the planning of those tactics at some point must include the captains of the individual ships if they are to be effective in defending the convoy.* So it is with the Enterprise. This used to be called participative management.

Some Great Entrepreneurs Fail the Transition

Some very successful entrepreneurial leaders are unable to survive the transition from small e to large E and to grow with the Enterprise as the CEO. Faced with a daunting task of running an entity where they can no longer reach out and touch every part of it, they often focus on areas which capitalize on their strengths and pay scant attention to other areas where they are weak without creating any provision for those weaknesses. Yet they keep their hands firmly on the steering wheel and the throttle, and subordinates are wary of encroaching on the boss's prerogatives. As a result, there is often no one watching large parts of the operation.

2.3 Balancing the Stakeholders' Interests

In Chapter 1 we stated that the integral manager considers all the stakeholders as they affect the management team's responsibilities. In this section I will strive to describe these forces, which are often in conflict. I will also suggest ways for effectively achieving balance and increasing the congruency of motivations among all classes of stakeholders.

We also said that an Enterprise is like a society within Society. It has a personality determined by at least some of its stakeholders. It is neither democratic nor, in modern times, totally autocratic. Its place in that continuum has a lot to do with how the business performs, grows and survives. History has shown again and again that productive innovation is stifled in an autocratic society. On the other hand, if all decisions are made *ad hoc* or by vote, you soon have total chaos. Like society, business enterprises need standards in order to discourage unproductive behavior. It is worth some effort to understand the motivating forces that influence the various stakeholders in an Enterprise.

The stakeholders and their motivations

In Chapter 1 we noted that there are at least six classes of stakeholders in a commercial profit-oriented Enterprise:
- Investors or shareholders,
- Senior management,
- Customers,
- Middle management,
- Employees, long-and short-term
- Suppliers

Each of these stakeholder classes has a different set of motivations with respect to the Enterprise and its management decision- making. Effective managers must understand these different forces and strike a proper balance among them.

A. Shareholders or investors

Shareholders have a single interest: return on their investment. This return comes in two forms: dividends on stock, and appreciation of the share value. If they believe that the return on this investment beats or will beat the returns that they could get in other investments, they stay. If not, they leave.

Since the trading of shares in a publicly held company takes place on the open market, investor interest and confidence is strongly influenced by the views of professional stock analysts, traders, and financial institutions that are the market- makers. This means, by and large, that shareholders are driven primarily by short-term, bottom-line results and much less by long-range growth. Many of the shareholders are institutional -- pension funds or other large entities -- who pick and reward their fund managers based on short-term results, with the possibility of large-volume transactions hinging on their view of the short-term return.

B. Senior management

The CEO of a major Enterprise is often thought of as perched at the pinnacle of a giant pyramid, wielding infinite power over his or her domain. I have not been in those shoes, so it would be presumptuous to say I fully understand the job. On the other hand, I have been close enough to what these individuals have to deal with to suggest that the popular perception is incomplete.

I think a more accurate representation would add another inverted pyramid above the CEO, as illustrated in Figure 2-1, sandwiching him or her between the apexes of the two pyramids. The board of directors is around the CEO at that pressure point, and depending on whether board members are helpful, passive, or adversarial, may be sharing the load or adding to it. Note which stakeholders are in that upper pyramid, and it is easy to see what forces are at work on the corporate management.

Executive management is measured and rewarded largely on short-term financial performance. Generally, a major part of their compensation is in the form of bonuses and options emphasizing the short-term bottom line that keeps Wall Street happy. Increasing shareholder value is a key part of their job and the value of those options increases accordingly. At the same time, keeping the stock price up helps protect against predatory takeover artists, who are aided and abetted by Wall Street investment bankers. While investment bankers may not be stakeholders per se, as deal makers they can often put a company in play for a takeover. Their interest is in a piece of the deal in a turnover, so they cannot be ignored.

A Corporate Stakeholders Model

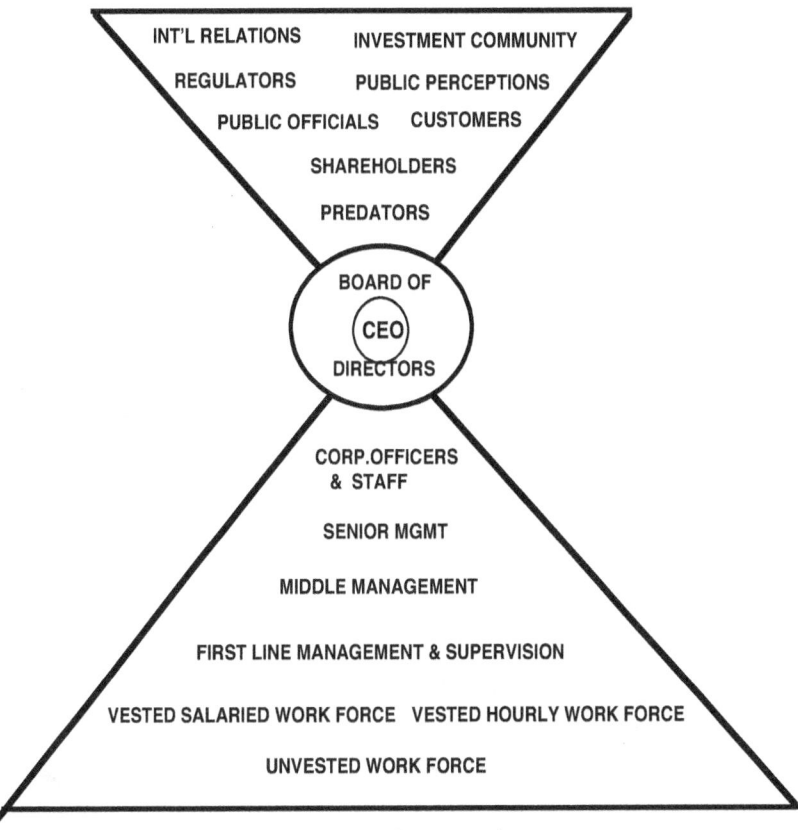

Figure 2-1 The Reality

Increasingly, because of this huge financial community influence, fads spawned by Wall Street analysts can unduly affect management decisions in an enterprise. Some of these are described in later chapters.

C. Customers

Customers may be a combination of short- and long-term, or simply short-term depending on their stake. Familiarity and trust are important to customers who feel that they are part of a long-term relationship. This is particularly true when they have been satisfied with the performance of what they purchased, whether a car or appliance or a major complex system. They are concerned about warranties, servicing and repair support for what they have acquired, or are continuing to buy many more units with a need for homogeneity in their inventory. Brand loyalty is real and is indicative of customers with the long-term view.

On the other hand, buying decisions are made on perceived value at the lowest price, and many customers never look past that parameter. This is particularly true of one-time buyers, buyers who are not concerned about future support, and as is prevalent in government, buyers who will not be around when the chickens come home to roost. In any case, continued customer satisfaction is a critical measure of the health of any Enterprise.

D. Middle management and employees with vested longevity

These employees are the primary stakeholders in the long-term viability of an Enterprise; middle management because of the opportunity to grow with attendant rewards, and long-time employees because of their vested benefits. This group is also the core intellectual capability and expertise of the Enterprise. Senior management must encourage and develop these individuals so they can grow into the future senior experts and management of the Enterprise.

E. The youngest employees

These stakeholders have little invested in future benefits, are very mobile, and usually are more concerned with immediate compensation and gratification than the long-term health of the Enterprise; but if they stay, they move into category D. Companies invest a lot of time, effort and money to attract young and educated employees trained in up-to-date methods in their respective fields. It is incumbent on management to build loyalty and trust among these new stakeholders.

F. Suppliers

Since often half of the value added to products comes from outside suppliers, they are significant stakeholders who depend on a level playing field and equity in their dealings with the Enterprise. Senior management establishes the climate that determines the standards for relationships with suppliers.

The Lesson to be Learned

It takes courageous and visionary senior management, willing to risk abuse and possibly monetary or career damage, to take the long view of the Enterprise in the face of today's short-term pressures. What seems wrong is for senior management not to be more concerned with what happens after their stewardship.

In my view, the successful CEO is one who achieves both short and long-term growth. A CEO who achieves high profitability over a five-year period by destroying his company's future is an abject failure. Incentives that focus only on stock price and measures of cash delivered this year are a serious threat to American industry. Yet, this is what the new breed in the investment community demands, and their influence is enormous, creating an equally enormous stress on the fabric of integrity within the Enterprise.

Is There a Solution to This Dilemma?

I believe that the best medicine for this malady is to ensure that the fabric of integrity within the Enterprise is strong enough to resist the stress of these external forces. This means that there must be contracts between levels of management, with financial objectives, that are bilateral and realistically negotiated at each step along the way. Promises must not be sought nor made at any level, which cannot be met without destroying the future. This is the environment defined in Chapter One.

As mentioned there, the behavior of management from the top to the lowest level establishes the environment of an Enterprise. What management teaches the Enterprise by the actions it takes and the behavior it tolerates far surpasses the significance of any words it utters. It can take years to undo the damage done by poor management. So, the challenge is to create a means of delegating management responsibility to capable lower-level leaders, inculcating the desired style of management integrity, while developing the feedstock for management succession to maintain the continuity of integrity for the future.

2.4 A Common Failure

The most common failure of top managers in companies large and small is the failure to recognize what their management team's job should be, and the creation of an organization structure that enshrines that failure so that no one else can confidently do their job. Although it's rarely admitted, organizations are often created with the intent to make the exercise of power and authority by top management easier, without considering organizational effectiveness and without involvement of subordinate managers. In reality, organizational structure often reflects the insecurity of the top management team, perhaps colored by a previous bad experience.

2.5 The Division of Management Responsibility

In order to start thinking about management interaction and how to organize effectively, we must first consider the appropriate division of management responsibility.

Delegation and Management Development

In any vibrant Enterprise, there is an insatiable need for effective managers. As with trees, new branches sprout, older branches die off and senior people move on to other endeavors. And sometimes people fail and need to be replaced. As a result, there are usually more opportunities than there are candidates. Properly managing managers and developing them is the best way to provide the feedstock to meet these management needs.

There are many ways to encourage the proper division of management responsibility, delegation, and the development of management talent. A common theme in all of them is the mutual setting of expectations and evaluation criteria, and the delegation of both responsibility and authority in an environment that embodies integrity. Once again, we are talking about bilateral contracts. Two concepts apply here:

A. *Management by objectives*[4] - as opposed to micromanagement. The idea behind management by objectives is to establish expectations jointly with your individual subordinates for the coming period -- usually a year. These expectations include where you want them to focus their efforts, what the constraints are, and what the degree of difficulty is. Agree on

---

[4] *Management by Objectives - A System of Management Leadership* by George S. Odiorne. Pitman Publishing 1965

the performance criteria for achievement and status reporting, then step back and let them do the job you have defined together. Delegate! Coach! Evaluate! But don't hover.

   B. Delegation with confidence. If you can't delegate to a subordinate manager or feel you must direct him or her to do things differently, one of you is in the wrong job. By directing, you have taken their responsibility, and should do one of two things-- take that person's place or find someone to whom you are willing to delegate.

Tolerating Dissent and Change

If management is to be truly participative, upper management must maintain an environment where members of the management team can voice their concerns and raise objections without fear. This does not require that management accept dissenting views, but it does require respecting them. Senior management often finds this concept threatening, but it should not be so. It often exposes information that can modify the proposed action in an advantageous way while eliminating the objection. Everybody wins. I'll say more about participative management later in the book.

In the next chapter, we will start to examine the roles and relationships associated with this division of management responsibilities within a high-integrity Enterprise. We will begin with project management because projects are the crucible where people and organizations and resources all come together in interdependent roles, and where leadership and the work environment can make or break the success of the endeavor. Almost all the issues of management and organization come into play in a project activity. As a result, the project or program provides us a model for the Enterprise.

Chapter 3 Projects and Planning
The Project Plan as a Foundation

3.0 Introduction to Projects

The first management model we will examine is the project or program management role. Let us define a project as the aggregated activities required to create a new product or to significantly revise an existing product. It can be just a few people working together to create some end product, or it can be a large-scale undertaking with thousands of people working to create a complex system. I arbitrarily define a program to be a grander scale of project, perhaps made up of many projects. I will use "project" and "program" interchangeably in this book because in fundamental terms, the scale defines the only difference.

Starting here seemed to make sense for several reasons. First, most start-up companies begin as single projects. In a single product enterprise, the project relationships tend to define the organization. Second, the relationships required to successfully plan and execute a project include virtually all disciplines and interfaces in an enterprise and thus provide a good model for discussing these issues.

This chapter will examine the project planning process and the relationships involved. The next chapter will deal with the project management roles and relationships among the various types of managers in the enterprise. In the process we will build a more specific image of the integral management environment.

3.1 Projects and Plans

In today's competitive environment, product technologies intended to meet a market need --with the possible exception of buttons and wire nails—require a development phase and then must transition into a production environment with a minimum of problems and expense. The total set of activities for creating the design, processes, facilities, and materials needed to reliably produce the product at a profitable cost is often called a project, and the orchestration of those activities is project management. The more complex the product, the more complex the project.

The foundation of the integrity of any project is project planning. The project plan defines the anatomy of the project, and is a fundamental tool for communication between the project management team and all the project participants. As such, planning evolves as decisions and strategies are selected, and continues to evolve in response to events as the project progresses.

When a new project is begun, usually those who will later implement production have great difficulty coping with the ambiguities of limited development definition. Much inter-action is required between the definers and the future producers for the project to get the level of definition needed and avoid gross error in scope. If the project plan is not done thoroughly as part of the pre commitment process, grave danger lies ahead. The type of commitment needed and its attendant risk to buyer and seller is an important subject that will be treated in detail in Chapter 12, *Contracts.*

3.2 The Project plan: Its Purpose, and Content

A project is like an auto trip on a holiday when all the gas stations are closed. Suppose we want to drive from Syracuse to Boston. What routes can we choose? How much fuel will we need? When do we need to arrive? When are we ready to leave? How fast can we drive? If there's an accident on the thruway, is there an alternate route? What if it snows? The fuel required is analogous to the cost of the project. The route and the transit time define the plan and the schedule. Your time to market is when you need to arrive in Boston. If you can't get there by then, there is no sense in making the trip.

A project or program plan is the basis for common understanding of the tasks required to accomplish all parts of the project. It is therefore the basis for commitments on cost, schedule, and performance of each part of the project.

The plan answers the questions: ***What*** is to be done, ***how*** it will be done, ***when*** the various elements of it will be done, ***who*** will do each of those elements, ***how many*** of what are needed, ***how much*** effort it will take, and ***why*** is it being done as planned?

When is the Project Plan Needed?

The initial project plan is needed not only before the project begins, but also before any firm commitments about it are made. While the production process for an ongoing product is repetitive with well-defined and understood processes, a new project involves redefining everything and traversing uncharted territory in many cases. New orders for an existing product can rely on an excellent database, and the innovations are usually limited to carefully controlled tweaking to avoid inadvertent change. The organizational tasks for new orders of an existing product are therefore well defined, and the planning is already in place. Note that an existing product is one currently being produced, or in inventory. It is <u>not</u> one that has been produced before, but is not currently being produced. (That category which can get you in considerable trouble lies somewhere in between.)

Who Should Create the Plan?

The ideal answer is that the people who have to execute the plan should create it. In complex projects with many interacting activities, integration is required. Therefore, a master schedule is generally needed with some ground rules to be used for common planning. The plan, then, is really a hierarchy of plans, which also shows the inter-dependency among them. Those who will make the commitments and perform the work for each of the activities should help create the plans for those activities.

How is a Project Plan Different Than a Business Plan?

A program or project plan is complementary to a business plan and provides the basis for validating it. The business plan, however, is normally aimed at the financial rationale for doing the project and the investment versus return on that investment, taking into account factors such as the market, the time value of money and risk etc. The project plan provides the data to validate or change assumptions about assets and resources needed, and time to break-even in the business plan.

Relation of Plan to Specifications or Other Requirements

A specification defines *what* is required in the end product. The spec, whether a buyer's document or a seller's document, is normally a requirements document invoked in the contract of sale. The plan, on the other hand, defines what activities will be required to provide the product that meets the spec and *how* it will be provided as a function of time. The plan is normally not a contract document. It is rather a description of intended approach that faces two directions. It tells the customer what the basis of quote was and therefore what to expect, and also tells those doing the work the approach that was assumed when the job was quoted. As such, the commitments made to the plan are internal contracts within the project. Because it is valuable for both purposes, some contracts may require delivery of that plan just for information. However, it is a living document that should be modified as the work progresses.

3.3 The Planning Process

Figure 3-1 maps the process of a typical project aimed at turning a market need into a cost-effective quality product. We start at the upper left of the chart where the need for the product is identified. Of course, getting to that defined need is itself a non-trivial process and a subject of separate study.

Product Synthesis and Definition

Here, we take it as a given that there is a need for the product with some desired attributes defined at least in principle. We move across the top of the chart to define the requirements for the product. What are the measures of goodness or effectiveness for the product? What are the attributes that maximize those measures? As shown by the arrows going both ways, this process is an iterative one.

The key word here is "tradeoffs." Remember that what we are after is customer satisfaction, and that means meeting the need at an attractive cost to the buyer. What must the product deliver as a minimum? What is additional capability worth? Operations research skills can be especially important here to evaluate the sensitivity of customer mission and cost requirements to the capabilities the company is able to offer. What can we provide? Is it feasible to make this product for the selling price the marketing experts say is needed? Do we have a distinguishing product concept? What is the competition able to deliver? In this critical phase of the project we are doing preliminary straw-man designs and straw man project plans -- checking feasibility and refining requirements.

THE PROCESS

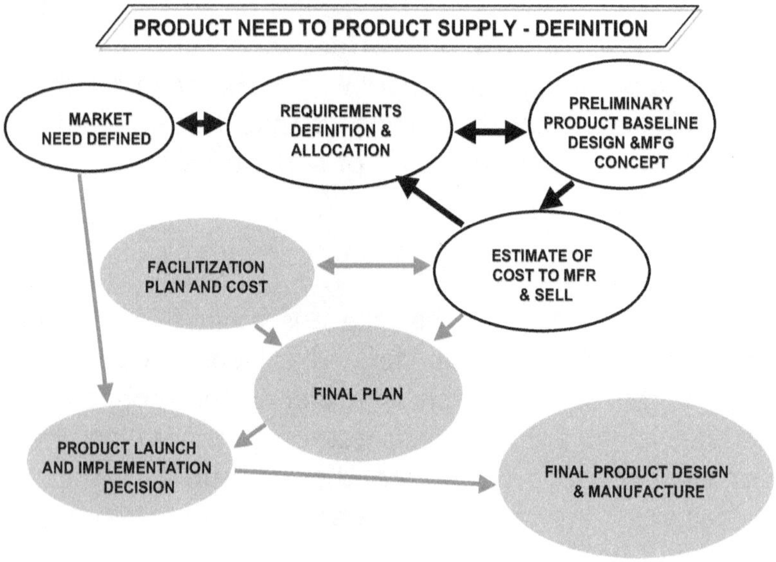

PRODUCT NEED TO PRODUCT SUPPLY - DEFINITION

MARKET NEED DEFINED

REQUIREMENTS DEFINITION & ALLOCATION

PRELIMINARY PRODUCT BASELINE DESIGN &MFG CONCEPT

FACILITIZATION PLAN AND COST

ESTIMATE OF COST TO MFR & SELL

FINAL PLAN

PRODUCT LAUNCH AND IMPLEMENTATION DECISION

FINAL PRODUCT DESIGN & MANUFACTURE

Figure 3-1

This is the phase where euphoria is a danger. When overly optimistic assessments are made, and the voices of reason are drowned out, bad things follow.

Defining the Approach

In Figure 3-2, the detailed project planning process, which is critical to success, starts at the upper right of the chart and flows down the diagonal to the lower left where a go/no-go decision must be made. Note that this planning process is also iterative and is going on in concert with the product definition.

THE PROCESS

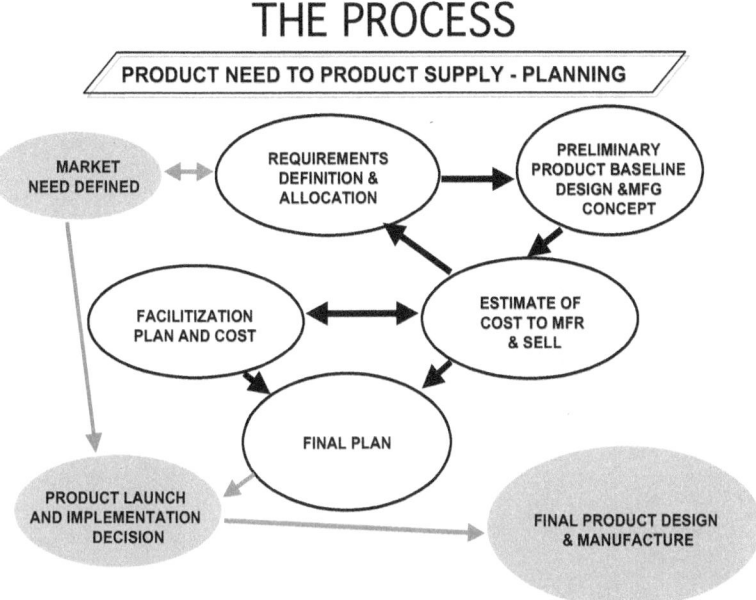

Figure 3-2

At the end of the planning process we know what our product strategy is; what the design approach is; what activities must occur; when they must occur; what facilities and resources will be needed to accomplish the plan; and we have a pretty good estimate of the cost and time it will take. If done collaboratively and with integrity, it is a plan that can be implemented. If this plan meets the criteria of the market need and is feasible as judged by the team and the final decision-maker, the project is launched.

Getting Buy-in

At this point more people generally join the team, and a major danger is that the newcomers have a tendency to disclaim all that has gone before, and reinvent the whole thing. How do we prevent this lack of ownership? The answer is simple, but not always easy. It is to get buy-in during the planning and concept phase from those who will implement the project.

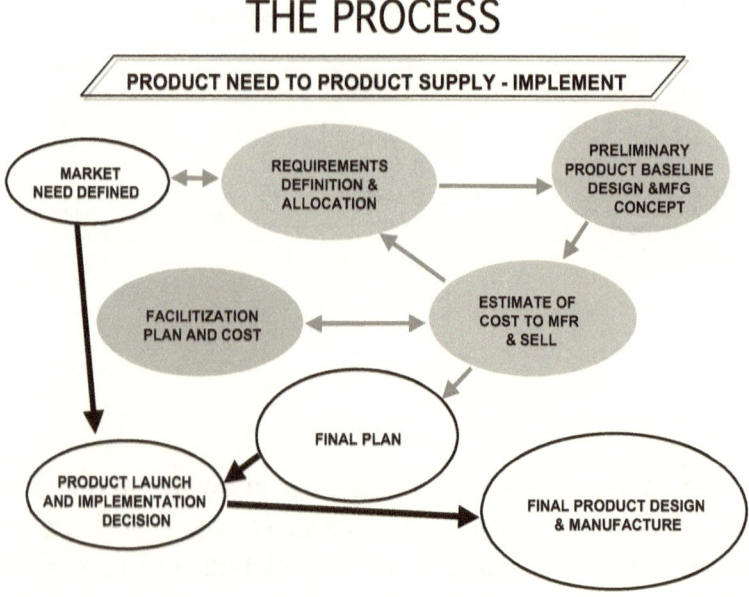

THE PROCESS

PRODUCT NEED TO PRODUCT SUPPLY - IMPLEMENT

Figure 3-3

One effective way to do this is with what is currently called an **integrated product team (IPT).** The IPT concept and concurrent engineering are discussed in more detail in Chapter 5. The key concept for successful IPTs is to get *empowered representatives* of all the disciplines that add value during the creation of the product *working together from the outset to define both the design and the plan.*

This includes the requirements definers, the design engineers, the test team, the buyers of materials and components, the manufacturing team and subcontractors, and the quality assessment, maintenance, logistics, and distribution folks who have to get it to the market. Make sure that they have a stake in the outcome. That is what ownership is about. Figure 3-3 shows the final steps in the decision process for accepting the baseline plan and buy in by those involved in the decision.

People are the Key and They Are Only Human

It should be evident that the most important ingredients in any project are people and how they interact to plan and execute the project. Since all of us have strengths and weaknesses, one key to successful projects is to bring the strengths together and compensate where there are weaknesses.

For example, the engineering activity is usually central to both the definition of the product and the planning for any successful product development, but engineers often suffer from one or both of two weaknesses. First, engineers are generally trained more to deal with things and ideas, not people problems. Second, many engineers don't like to commit to a plan until they have finished the engineering. The "I'll tell you when it's ready" approach may give the engineer a feeling of security, but it is anything but collaborative. If you are the person who has to provide the manufacturing tooling by a certain time, or the building where the product will be manufactured, you can't accept that answer. The effective process is to consider all of the other members of this collaborative team as your customers. For a plan to be realistic and successful, commitments must be made and then met. In short, both the design and the planning must have *integrity.*

Optimum Usually Isn't!

Beware of people who bring you "optimum" solutions or plans. Optimums are a mathematical concept with limited use outside that field of study.

This is an important thought that applies to projects, designs, organizations, and almost every other facet of life. What you are usually offered with this engaging adjective is a sub-optimized plan or solution that ignores some important parameters. Check it out! There is no such thing as the perfect or optimum plan or implementation!

3.4 Implementing the Plan

Even the best planning cannot anticipate every eventuality. That is why a plan is a living document that will be modified several times during the execution of the project. This modification must be done in a controlled fashion so everyone involved is reading from the same page, so to speak. An effective way to do this is to use program baseline designations such as "A", "B", "C" for major block changes. Interim decisions or incremental changes can be documented via individual coordinated memos. When significant re-planning is required, a block change to the baseline can also incorporate the incremental changes.

Project implementation management roles and relationships are discussed in detail in Chapter 4. Later chapters address the specific disciplines that I believe are required to implement a project.

If it Can Happen, It Will! If It Can't Happen, It Also Will!

As this suggests, sometimes, in spite of the best-laid plans and good execution, something unexpected and ugly occurs that demands decisive corrective action. Suffice it to say here that if you are the project manager, while the team focuses on executing the plan, you must be looking ahead, watching for trouble and asking yourself where the risks are, and "what if?" Some contingency plans and back-ups can be implemented for only $1.98 more, figuratively speaking. They can often save you many times what they cost.

An observation or experience in project management inspired some wag to define the phases of a typical project. Shown here, these phases often apply -- even to successful projects, which may have some bumps and surprises along the way.

- **CONFIDENT OPTIMISM**
- **DISILLUSIONMENT**
- *PANIC*
- **SEARCH FOR THE GUILTY**
- **PUNISHMENT OF THE INNOCENT**
- *Praise & Honors to the Non-Participants*

Somewhere between phase three and five is where the project manager often gets replaced.

These are the times that test the mettle and integrity of managers. Management by wishful thinking doesn't get you there. It helps to maintain some sense of humor and irony at those times. Here are a couple of apt one-liners I have come across.

"Today is the first day of the rest of the trouble." - author unknown
"I only dread one day at a time." Charlie Brown to Linus at the wall in "Peanuts" by Charles Schultz.

Just be sure these don't become your real philosophy.

3.5 Estimating the Impact of Program Changes

We know that funding, whether internal or external to the enterprise, is the fuel that shapes the program plan. The development of the details of a program baseline plan involves a great deal of effort in task and resource planning by all members of the implementing project team. These detailed plans and the means to monitor performance against them are discussed in chapter 8 on cost management.

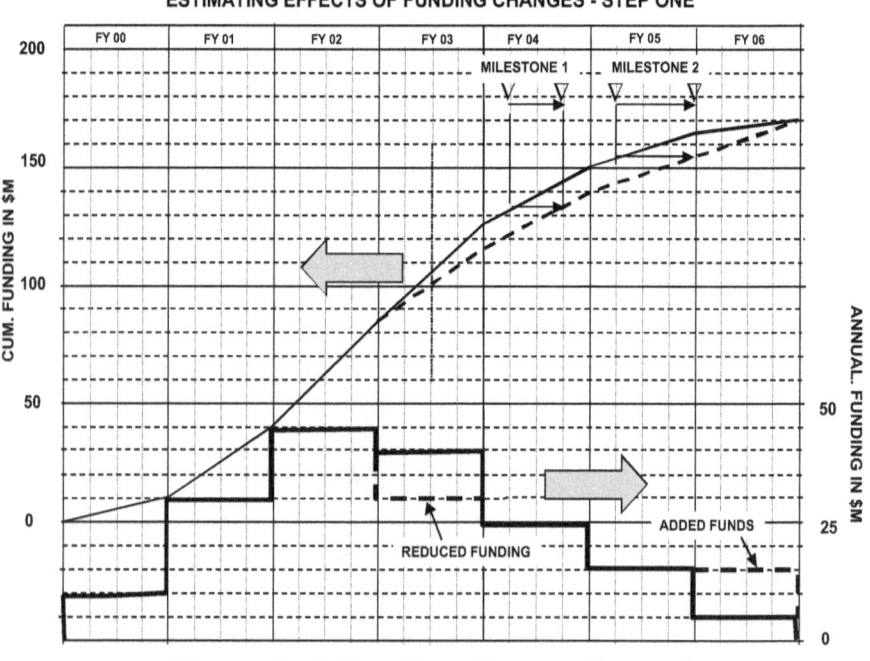

Figure 3-4 Funding Change Example

Given that detailed baseline, when program changes are required, it is almost always necessary to estimate the impact on cost and schedule before doing a detailed re-plan. The following discussion offers a method for assessing these impacts by using the current well-defined baseline as a point of departure.

Figure 3-4 shows a sample program funding profile by fiscal year along with a cumulative funding curve. Proposed funding profile changes are also shown. We can evaluate the effect of a funding reduction or increase in any given year. The example shows a reduction in FY '03, which is not restored until FY '06, as shown in the lower curve against its scale on the right side of the chart. The upper curve with its scale on the left side of the chart is the cumulative funding of the project.

The dashed curve shows the effect of reduced cum funding and allows evaluation of how various milestones will be approximately affected based on the principle that the cum funding up to the time of that milestone determines when that milestone can occur. We can see in this example that key milestone 1 in FY '04 will slip 6 months and key milestone 2 in FY05 will slip 9 months.

This technique as the first step allows a rebalance of all tasks in the project to determine the minimum overall impact, but does not account for the cost effects of moving effort down-stream or the effects of constraining labor profiles both in house and at suppliers. Once step one is done for each portion of the project, the effects of time shifting of resources can be determined as described in figure 3-5.

A slip in a key milestone can occur either due to a funding limitation, or a problem in a prior activity that forces a delay in downstream tasks.

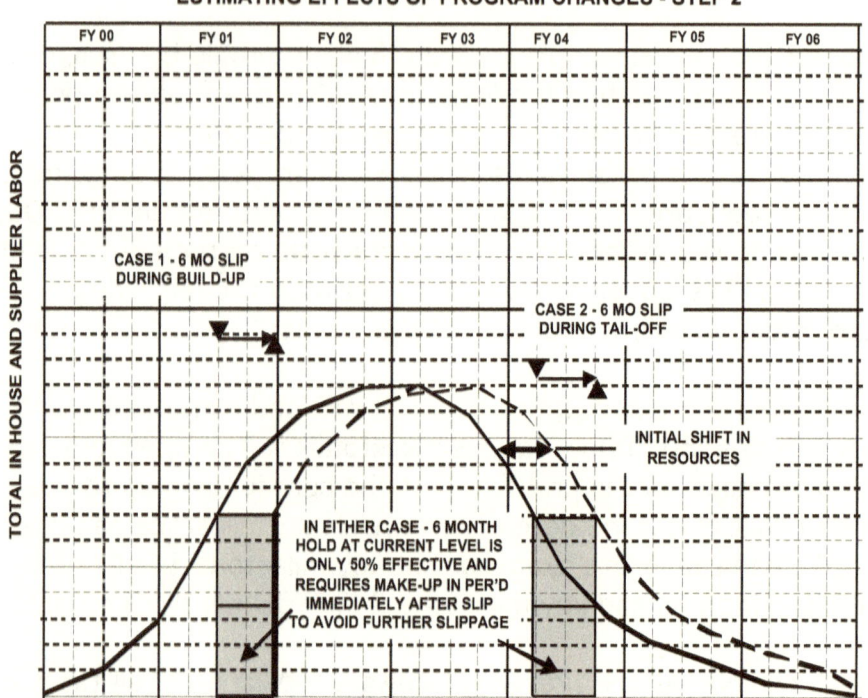

Figure 3-5 Effect of Slips on Resources

The two cases shown in figure 3-5 have different effects because they occur at different phases of the activity. In case 1, the slip has occurred during the build-up of headcount on the project. In this case, when the slip is initiated, headcount is frozen at the level on board in house and at all suppliers at the time the slip occurs.

As a result, less funding is required during the last half of the fiscal year '01, and in fiscal year '02, represented by the difference between the original labor profile (the solid curve), and the dashed shifted curve. This funding must be added back in subsequent years as reflected by the six month shift in all downstream effort, remembering to account for economic escalation associated with the shift in resources to later years.

However, reassignment and rehiring, shortages from prior delayed work and other disruption factors, will cause the work accomplished during the 6 month slip as a rule of thumb to be only 50% effective toward meeting future milestones during this period. In order to prevent the overall remaining activity from further slippage, this 50% lost productivity must be added to the total funding and specifically in the period immediately following the slip -- FY 02 in case one.

Case 2 provides a different situation where the slip occurs during the tail-off of labor. Since the effort to complete requires the same area under the to go curve after the slip, the headcount must again be frozen at this level when the slip begins. In this case, the same rule of thumb applies where the added effort during this time will be 50% effective toward accomplishing down-stream milestones and therefore only 50% of this added effort during the slip will increase total project cost. As before the pricing of shifted resources must also account for any resource cost escalation associated with the time shift.

The methodology of these two charts is what I call the principle of optimum baselines, which premises that a baseline program has been planned and is being implemented in efficient fashion and any change which does not reduce scope is a perturbation which will have an adverse impact.

3.6 Conclusion

I believe that the recipe for success in managing a project is summarized below. The elements are simple and obvious, but that doesn't mean they are followed. It always amazes me how uncommon common sense really is. Your job as an Integral manager will be to practice these principles consistently and encourage them in others.

THE SECRET FORMULA FOR SUCCESS

- UNCOMMON SENSE
- UNCOMPROMISING INTEGRITY
- MAKE TIME YOUR ALLY, NOT YOUR ENEMY: PLAN!
- GET TEAM OWNERSHIP OF THE PLAN
- YOU MAKE LUCK. IT ISN'T SOMETHING THAT HAPPENS TO YOU
    - EXPECT THE UNEXPECTED. YOU WILL RARELY BE DISAPPOINTED
    - FOLLOW YOUR CONVICTIONS, BUT OFTEN ASK "WHAT IF?"

Remember, as a manager, you will not be the only one who makes the project succeed; the people who work for you will. You don't have to master every technical discipline involved in creating the project; you don't have to review and approve every single action in the course of development; <u>but you must create an environment where people are empowered to do their jobs with integrity.</u> Communicate your expectations of them as clearly as you can, give them the authority to do the job, and hold them accountable. Coach them, lead them, make decisions when necessary, but let them help make the whole team succeed.

In this chapter we have discussed the underlying philosophy of sound project management. In the next chapter we will examine the details of management interrelationships when a project or program becomes large enough to involve multiple organizations within a larger Enterprise. At that point we will see how some of these principles are implemented.

Chapter 4 Project Management

Relationships

Roles of Program Management and Functional Organization Management

4.0 Introduction

An Enterprise that has organized to support several major customers or product lines usually appoints "Program" or "Project" managers dedicated to meeting each customer's requirements. Usually, much of the work is performed by functional organizations that have expertise needed across many programs. I differentiate "Program" from "Project" somewhat arbitrarily on the basis of size, scope, and internal vs. external customer.

4.1 Purpose

This chapter describes the organizational relationships that I believe apply in the conduct of business, with particular emphasis on the role of the program manager as he or she relates to the customer, functional management, and general management within the Enterprise. (Functional managers and organizations in an Enterprise are defined here as those that have an activity verb as part of their title. Examples are Engineering, Manufacturing, Procurement, Marketing, Shipping and Receiving, Quality Assurance, Accounting, etc.). The context of this discussion is a complex project or program where substantial new development is required.

It is important to keep in mind that customer/contractor relationships exist at all levels of a program -- not just between the company and the ultimate customers. The program manager will act as customer to functional organizations performing work on the program, much as if the functional organizations were outside subcontractors. Therefore, it is vital that the program manager and the functional managers negotiate a contract that is realistic and achievable, and that both sides commit to this contract.

4.2 Program Management Role

In preparing for a competitive or non-competitive business opportunity, it is incumbent on the company management to designate a proposal manager, who may also be the designated program manager. This individual will normally be chosen on the basis of his or her ability to organize pre-proposal activities, lead a proposal effort, conduct negotiations, and implement the work if the competition is successful. A small staff, experienced in these activities, forms the nucleus of the proposal manager's organization. The team will also include representatives from all activities that will be involved in implementation if the proposal is accepted.

The Program Manager's Charter

When our model Enterprise undertakes to develop and deliver a major product, a Program Manager is selected by senior management to act as the agent of both the customer to the company and the company to the customer. I like to think of the Program or Project manager as the General Contractor within the company and the chief advocate for his or her program. This role is to assure that: 1) An equitable business relationship is established in a contract that defines the work to be done; 2) A mutually agreed-to cost is established for the conduct of the effort, and 3) The necessary resources are brought to bear to accomplish the work in accordance with that contract.

In the typical development job, the developing Enterprise creates a product disclosure. This data includes the necessary analyses, simulations, hardware, software, and tests to prove that the product-- when built in accordance with the design documents, tools and processes described in that disclosure -- will perform the required function in accordance with the requirements of the contract.

Program Management Office

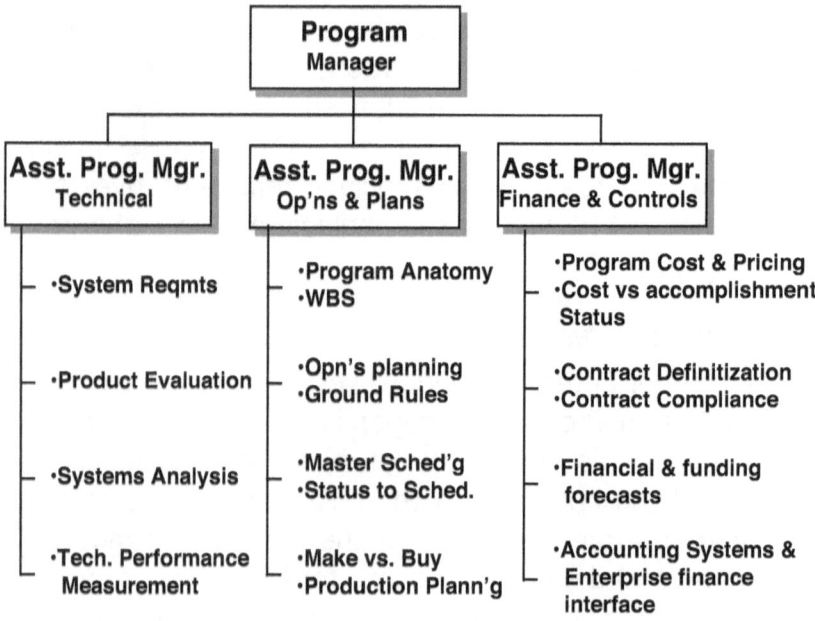

Figure 4-1 Typical Program Office Organization

In the multi project model, the Enterprise program manager relies on the functional engineering organization for creating and validating the design part of the product disclosure. But there is more to the product disclosure than the design. The production or operations organizations have the responsibility for creating and validating the procurement, production processes, and quality assurance portions of the product disclosure. I use the term "operations" to define all those repetitive activities that create the end product.

Figure 4-1 shows a typical major program management organization with three deputies, or assistant program managers (APMs) reporting to the program manager. The major program manager delegates responsibilities to these APMs and individual members of the program management team, but they are acting on behalf of the program manager.

In this multi project model, each program manager relies on the functional engineering organization for creating and validating the design part of the product disclosure. The production or operations organizations have the responsibility for creating and validating the procurement, production processes, and quality assurance portions of the product disclosure. I use the term "operations" to define all those repetitive activities that create the end product.

Assistant Program Managers

One APM position is shown as the *Assistant Program Manager - Technical.* This individual is the chief technical officer of the program. The technical system requirements for the product and evaluation of what is to be provided to meet those requirements are this individual's job. The "system requirements" part of systems engineering reports to this position, as do the operations analysis, and technical performance measurement functions.

A second APM, shown in Figure 4-1 as the *Assistant Program Manager - Operations and Plans,* is typically responsible for what I will call "program anatomy." The contract delivery requirements usually define the need dates for the products to be provided. Therefore, the program anatomy is largely determined by the lead times of activities necessary to build and deliver the product by the required date given the design documentation, plus the time to design and develop that documentation. Various ground rules, based on program considerations such as risk and contract constraints, may govern those activities. Knowledgeable about how the product will be produced, the APM *Operations and Plans,* is generally responsible for master scheduling, the work breakdown structure (see Chapter 7), operations planning, and the program milestones and statusing system for reporting progress and accomplishment.

In our model program organization, we believe that it is prudent to provide checks and balances to protect the fiduciary responsibilities of the Enterprise to its shareholders. To do this, we provide the program manager with an expert assistant in the financial management aspects of the activity.

This person, who is shown in Figure 4-1 as the *Assistant Program Manager - Finance and Controls* is responsible for assuring that the financial and contract commitments are understood, proper pricing methods are used, and that controls are in place to measure costs incurred and progress of the work. This individual reports to the program manager, but also to the Enterprise CFO, assuring both independent assessment and necessary support from the Enterprise financial accounting organization during all phases of the program.

Program Responsibilities by Program Phase

As the program authority within the company, the program manager is responsible to general management for assuring that an equitable relationship exists between the company and the customer. He or she is responsible for the initial definition of the program in enough detail to allow the proper company resources to be assigned. This definition is often necessary for the proposal itself, as well as for the execution of contractual effort where definition and interpretation of contract requirements with respect to task, performance, cost and schedule must be provided.

The program manager is responsible for seeing that the program definition is compatible with the funding plan on a multi-year basis where applicable. He or she is responsible for negotiating commitments with responsible functional managers along with securing the resources to fulfill these commitments.

A. Preparing for a Competition and Proposing

In the pre-proposal period, the program management team is responsible for assuring that the proper work is done to enable writing a winning proposal. They are expected to have sufficient insight into the nature of the task or procurement to provide mature leadership, as well as recommendations where management support is required for:

1) the amount of pre-proposal activity that should be authorized in view   of the size and worth of the procurement.
2) the kinds of talent that must be committed to prepare the proposal.
3) recommendations on strategy for both winning and implementing.

During the pre-proposal and proposal periods, the program manager is responsible for all activities and for assuring that the necessary resources are brought to bear. As in other phases of program management, he or she is expected to draw on functional organizations as required to prepare the proposal in sufficient technical and business depth.

Also, during the pre-proposal period, it is vital to determine what components of the product will be developed or produced by suppliers rather than internally as this will form the basis for the program plan and identify the types of resources required. This is called a make/buy strategy, and considers such factors as the skill-set and the cost structure of the Enterprise. The program manager is responsible for the make/buy plan, and must make decisions based on what is necessary to win and perform well on the program. The make/buy plan needs to encompass the engineering, test, manufacturing, operations, and services functions. While the program manager is responsible for the make/buy plan, and must make decisions based on what is necessary to win and perform well on the program, this is not a unilateral responsibility. Because there are often Enterprise policy considerations involved, the program manager must coordinate with the functional organizations and get agreement on the plan. The program manager must be prepared to justify the decisions concerning the make or buy plan. to general management.

B. Program Definition

Program definition requires the formulation of a program plan, including a master schedule, in sufficient detail to identify the key events for all required effort. It also requires an understanding of the interrelationships of tasks and milestones based on the objectives and characteristics of the program. From this understanding a program "anatomy" can be derived, starting from end-item delivery, and working backwards through all phases of production, development, and initial system definition.

In general, this task of system definition requires the efforts of people who have been through similar development programs and who are familiar with the types of lead times, schedule interactions and constraints that will influence the program anatomy. This expertise will often be centralized in a Program Plans and Controls organization. This organization will provide support for the program definition to each program in accordance with the program manager's guidelines and approval. It will also serve as the focal point for overall program status information, both to the program manager and to general management.

In the formative phases of a program, the program manager must strive to assure that optimism, either within the company or within the customer's ranks, is not allowed to damn the program with unacceptable technical and budgetary constraints. This means understanding what is required in performance and methodology to meet customer needs and how much it is worth to the customer to exceed the requirements, and matching these parameters up in a consistent set. Ideally, it means having a time-phased should-cost estimate with funding coverage. Because of the typical budget cycle, the program manager should be thinking at least 18 months ahead of everyone else.

As a general rule, the program manager should be in a position to know what should be done in a given situation, to make recommendations, and to be responsive to the customer's reaction to those recommendations. The program manager's primary task is to assure the program's success and the customer's success. The program manager must assume the customer has not planned far enough ahead and therefore should prepare and provide recommendations to help the customer's planning. At the same time, the program manager should not be so foolhardy as to assume that the customer does not know what it needs.

C. Funding Planning

The program manager is responsible for understanding the customer's or potential customer's budget plans and funding constraints. These will be used as a yardstick to determine both the viability of proposed or planned efforts and the program's success. The program manager may and should, where possible, influence and assist the customer in the formulation of those budgets. It is therefore incumbent upon the program manager, in the formulation of the initial estimates, to prepare a "should-cost" estimate, taking into consideration past performance on similar tasks, the effects of inflation using realistic assumptions, and differences in task complexity.

Every major system, no matter how complex, can be broken down into elements, which are similar to elements of other previous systems. The funding plan is expected to provide sufficient front-loading and allowance for unforeseen events. Therefore, rough-order-of-magnitude program cost estimates should be conservative, meaning that any subsequent refinement of the numbers will be smaller.

D. Definition and Commitment of Resources

The program manager is responsible to general management for assuring that company commitments are be met. To do this, he or she must assure that the necessary financial resources to do the job are made available and that the company resources are properly employed. This demands a continuity from definition through negotiation of the contract and, subsequently, through the period of performance on the contract.

Having defined the program anatomy and proposal ground rules, then, the program manager must review them with the functional organizations that will do the work, resolving any disagreements prior to the proposal.   These ground rules may well include a set of cost and performance targets based on knowledge of how much the customer wishes to spend, how much capability it wishes to buy, and the competitive environment.   This implies that there may be varying degrees of risk associated with these cost and performance targets.

The program manager defines what must be done at each stage of the program, starting with the pre-proposal activity.   In 95 percent of the cases, he or she will not define how the work to be done, but will rely on functional organizations to define this within their functional expertise and responsibility.   The program manager retains veto rights for his program -- a responsibility that is not to be taken lightly.

E. Negotiation of Tasks and Resources Prior to Contract Negotiations

Given a set of program definitions and proposal ground rules, the program manager must negotiate with the organizations that will perform the work to arrive at an equitable contract during the proposal activity.   The word "contract" is used here, because the functional organization is to be considered much as a subcontractor would be -- and the contract is every bit as binding. It requires a clear understanding and agreement on the degree of technical, schedule and cost risk embedded in the commitments.

It requires a definition of tasks in sufficient depth to ensure that the job can be done for the money proposed at the recognized confidence factors.   It follows, then, that the work breakdown structure must identify the work to be done and provide meaningful cost allocation within those elements.   While the cost accumulations structure need not duplicate the work breakdown structure, it is very important that they be a consistent set compatible with the job from both a definition and a control standpoint.

Agreements on tasks and resources, once signed by the responsible manager, are commitments expected to be met. The manager's performance in meeting these commitments will be a primary yardstick of job performance. The extent of known risk to meeting these commitments will of course be recognized in the overall assessment of the manager's performance. It is also important to remember that the commitment is not just the functional manager's, but the program manager's as well. A program manager who makes arbitrary cuts in proposed effort without getting the agreement of those who quoted, and who will do the work, will end up carrying the banner with no army when the contract is signed.

Where subcontractor effort is required, commitments are needed from those subcontractors based on scope in the same manner as if they were an organization within the company. Agreements should be documented and signed by the subcontractor, the committing buying organization and the accepting program manager.

F. Risk Assessment and Mitigation

When the proposal is ready to be submitted to the customer, the contractor will hold an Enterprise Management Review. The purpose of this review is to get final approval to submit the proposal, to discuss the risks and what approaches are planned to mitigate those risks. Above all, in a high integrity Enterprise, it is the time that senior management of the Enterprise "gets in the boat" with the program manager and the proposal team. Any issues that remain should be addressed and dispositioned. This review must occur long enough before the submittal date to allow for changes that result from it, or Enterprise senior management will not get in the boat.

Programs should be planned on a realistic basis -- not on a "no-mistakes" basis. There should be time in the schedules to allow for the unforeseen and for corrections when things go wrong. There should be resources planned for correcting designs, repeating tests, repair or replacement of parts or assemblies, developing replacement sources of supply, etc. The difference between the "no- mistakes" resources and the actually expected resources will provide the initial management reserve; this reserve must not be allocated when the program resources are budgeted.

G. Allocation of Resources

In the allocation of resources for the performance of work, whether contract activity, independent development, or bid and proposal effort, the same negotiation process should occur. In the allocation of tasks and the funding of independent development work or other discretionary funded tasks, the same "subcontractor" approach applies: the functional organization is the subcontractor. There should be agreement and documentation of the task and resources required, together with a schedule of completion for each element. The organization doing the work, as well as the program manager, must sign off on this contract.

In the case of contract funds, it is expected that agreement will be reached based on the proposal ground rules as modified by contract negotiations. It is therefore incumbent on the program manager to document changes in scope and resource reduction agreements accepted during the course of the negotiations and in-house preparation of "best and final" offers. A representative from each functional "doing" organization, with the authority to speak for the organization manager, should participate in contract negotiations to justify raw resource requirements and technical effort.

H. Determination of System Worth

Before a decision to pursue a new program, and during the conduct of the program, It is incumbent upon the prospective program manager to conduct evaluations of the worth of his or her program opportunity objectively. In the case of government programs, this means worth to the country, to the customer, and to the company. To do this, the program manager normally relies on a cadre of system analysts. However, the final decision must come from the program manager, who along with general management, must ultimately answer questions of system worth.

The program manager is expected to support an appropriate level of systems analysis to develop the models and tools necessary to answer these questions when they arise. Since systems analysis requirements tend to fluctuate by program, the basic analytical disciplines are often centralized in a functional organization to serve all programs. It is hoped that this will level the workload and maximize cross-fertilization in capability, techniques and study results.

4.3 The Role of the Functional Organization

The Internal Subcontractor Relationship

In my model of a multi-program Enterprise, program offices are the "general contractors" within the Enterprise who "subcontract" functional work such as engineering, test, and manufacturing to existing capable organizations within the Enterprise. They do not create separate projectized organizations other than those required for program management itself, unless special circumstances approved by general management require it.

A vital element of this subcontracting arrangement is the delegation of responsibility and authority for management of technical, schedule and cost performance for the job subcontracted. This relationship, as previously described, requires definition of the job starting with the proposal and mutual agreement on the resources required to accomplish it. Budget must be planned and visible for the term of the task to allow the functional organizations to do a proper job of task and manpower planning.

Implicit in this arrangement is the requirement that the functional organizations provide the technical and management excellence needed to fulfill their commitments. The functional manager negotiates the job and the resources with the program manager and is then held accountable for meeting this commitment. He or she must assure the assignment of needed talent and resources, plan and organize activities, assure clear assignment of responsibility for tasks and hardware, and reviews and approve the output. He or she is expected to provide guidance, when needed, both to the functional organization's representative to the program and to the program manager. In short, the functional manager is a team member who is contractually bound to the program, and must be ready and willing to be a member of any project team.

The second necessary condition is in management's commitment to the employees. When an employee from a functional organization is assigned to and co-located with a program, there must be no "out of sight, out of mind" situation. The functional organization manager must stay abreast of what the employee is doing and how he or she is performing. Performance evaluations should be joint efforts between the program manager and the functional organization manager. The functional organization manager must also recognize that the employee's assignment is a binding commitment -- there can be no unilateral actions to change assignments.

With these guarantees in place, it should not matter where an employee reports on the organization chart. The commitment is to the program, not to a particular organization.

The Concept of Subsystem Manager

When the product mix of an Enterprise has common technologies required to implement the spectrum of product lines, those disciplines and technologies are probably best grouped in functional organizations that would support all products. In particular where design and development are required, engineering is generally organized along functional capabilities and expertise (i.e., mechanical, electrical,) to match the end-product anatomy and is the initial formulator of solutions to meet the end-product requirements. In our model, an individual first level manager in engineering is assigned "ownership" for the successful conduct of the development and production of each major end item or group of items that relate or function together. In our model this individual is called a subsystem manager.

This section describes the assignment of responsibility to, and the authority of, an individual manager within the organization who takes the ownership of a subsystem or equipment to assure and be accountable for: 1) development of the equipment or subsystem to meet the need specified; 2) providing that item at the time and place required in a condition suitable for use as intended by the requirements at a cost consistent with expectations . This manager is called the *subsystem manager.*

Assignment of Subsystem Management Responsibility to Engineering

The subsystem manager has responsibility for determining and implementing the design solution to meet all of the contractual requirements of the program for his or her subset of the product. Because the engineering definition is required before most of the other activities of the organization can begin, engineering normally must take the lead as the subsystem manager.

Subsystem Manager's Role and Responsibilities

The subsystem manager's responsibility goes further than simply establishing the design definition. Since the design definition initiates much of the activity of the rest of the organization in increasing magnitude as the program matures, the subsystem manager must continue to lead throughout the design process. He or she is also responsible for certifying that the necessary analysis, test and verification work has been done to assure that the end-item will meet the program requirement, whether it is a flight test or readiness for production. Thus, the subsystem manager has responsibility for all development testing and specimens needed to establish design confidence prior to release of the design. Because he or she must certify the end item's readiness for use, this manager is also responsible for evaluation of test results from end-item configuration hardware and software built to released documentation by suppliers or in-house.

He or she must consider the subsystem as a product that must be manufactured, tested and fielded, and try to anticipate downstream problems. He or she must participate with manufacturing, product assurance and the field in production and usage that should be considered in the design of that subsystem. He or she may, and often will take the lead in problem resolution-with other implementing organizations such as manufacturing or procurement to ensure achievement of the subsystem goals.

Subsystem Manager's Role in Subcontract Management

When the subsystem manager's end-items are designed and built by a subcontractor, his or her overall role is nearly unchanged. The subcontract management team approach is discussed in detail in Chapter 5, along with the roles of each Enterprise organization. The subsystem manager is still the "owner" of the design, responsible personally or through a delegate for the technical direction of the subcontractor activities needed to secure development and production of the items for which he or she is responsible.

However, there is a fundamental difference between managing in-house design and manufacture and subcontracted design and manufacture. In the in-house case, the Enterprise infrastructure provides planning, status, integrated master schedule commitments, etc. When a supplier is to do this work, that subcontractor must provide the equivalent activity and data. The Enterprise subsystem manager must still be fully aware of this situation and assure that the activities are performed and the data is supplied. This is accomplished through the contract statement of work and through the personal attention and knowledge of the subsystem manager and the rest of the subcontract management team.

Each subsystem manager will designate an individual who has responsibility for each subcontract under their purview. This designee is delegated subsystem management responsibility and will serve as the chairman of the management team for that subcontract through production design freeze. The subcontract management team will include designated members from materiel as subcontract administrator and business manager, product assurance for quality requirements, program controls where warranted and the program office for program requirements and integration. Other representatives from test, manufacturing and other areas may be required depending on the subcontract.

This subcontract management team is, in effect, a miniature program management function to integrate the management and performance assessment of that subcontracted effort. The subsystem manager thus functions as a program manager for his subsystem.

4.4 Organizational Relationships

Recall that in this management model, the program manager acts like a general contractor "subcontracting" the work (other than program requirements and integration) to entities that are skilled in the necessary disciplines to best perform the work required. Those "subcontractors" are the functional organizations. Normally, there are several programs going on at the same time as depicted in Figure 4-2. Moreover, within a given program a functional organization will have several major jobs on which to perform.

We have said that the ideal organization is configured to delegate the responsibility for the planning and conduct of work. Thus, it can be performed by organizations with the logical combinations of skills and resources to be accountable for and accomplish the work with minimum conflict with other activities.

The work can be divided in several ways. This requires clear delineation of authority and interfaces with respect to that work. Typically this means a division of the work into similar types of functions and skills or by facility proprietorship, or to provide required checks and balances.

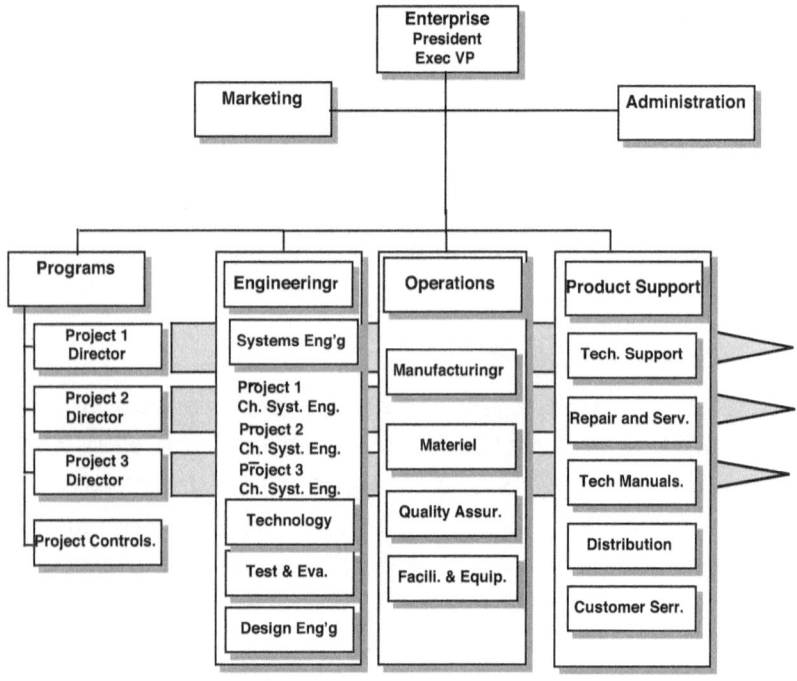

Figure. 4-2

In the operations branches (manufacturing, materiel, product assurance, field support) for instance, the organization tends to be by the type of work to be done or the location where it is to be done. In Engineering, on the other hand, it is end-product oriented because the disciplines required generally relate to the functions that the product performs rather than the process needed to produce it. Finally, test and validation functions may be assigned to a separate organization to preserve the objectivity of this function.

Every organization that adds value to the product during its creation and lifetime should be represented in all phases of the planning as well as implementation of the project. Ownership must be established for every activity involved. For example, make vs. buy decisions must have buy-in from the operations organizations. To assure that this happens, a make vs. buy evaluation is usually required by general management of the enterprise and chaired by the senior manager of operations. Care must be taken to assure that those decisions are based on sound business grounds and not driven by anyone's bias or ambitions.

The end result of the planning process should be signed contracts between the program manager and all "subcontractors," both internal and external. The terms of those contracts should identify all the resources needed to fulfill the contracts, including any new facilities or capabilities to be acquired.

4.5. Performance against Commitments

The contracts just discussed between functional and program managers are *commitments*. A commitment made is a commitment expected to be met.

While it is recognized that problems may arise in the course of the execution of a job that may prevent a commitment from being met, every manager is expected to have visibility into the performance of his work. Thus, if a commitment appears to be in jeopardy, it must be made visible to the program manager to whom that commitment was made with sufficient lead-time to allow corrective action to be taken. This means having a meaningful plan for the work to be done, with meaningful measures of accomplishment and due-dates agreed to by all affected organizations.

It is unacceptable for a commitment to be found incomplete on the day it is due -- whether it is a scheduled event, a task completion, or an action item. On the other hand, where situations beyond the control of the responsible individual will result in a commitment not being met, the timely reporting and visibility of that condition is of vital importance. This is a measure of a manager's planning and control of the activities for which he is responsible. The same relationship must be maintained between the program manager, as the company's agent, and the customer. While no one likes bad news, it is much easier to take when there is time to react and take contingent action.

4.6 Overarching Disciplines Support Program Integrity

To be successful, any program or project must implement certain integration functions to tie the project together and assess its progress. . We call these overarching disciplines. To assure the integrity of the project, these disciplines provide checks and balances among the organizations involved. Often the people assigned to their project do not appreciate the need for these disciplines; sometimes their managers don't, either. But to ignore them is to almost assure failure.

A program or project can be described as three kinds of activities generally occurring in parallel. They are: 1) Program Definition and Planning; 2) Program Implementation; and 3) Program Evaluation. The overarching disciplines fit into one or more of these three categories and are applied across the project. The expertise for applying them usually resides in functional specialty organizations as direct support to the program management team, as discussed below. A more detailed discussion of the methodology involved in these integrating disciplines is provided in Chapter 7, Integration Arts.

Systems Engineering

A. Requirements and Evaluation

This activity is really the technical arm of the program manager, disseminating and allocating program requirements to the design activities, and then evaluating the ability of the design to meet those requirements

B. Design Integration

This is the design activity that establishes interfaces and allocates functionality among the segment design teams of the product.

Product Safety, Quality, Reliability and Maintainability

This activity applies the expertise of the end application and ultimate user of the product and establishes the philosophy for minimizing the user's cost of ownership. It audits the product during its design to assure that these elements are included in the product as it evolves.

Integrated Test and Evaluation

This activity is the independent test conductor and evaluator during development. The integrated test program plan gathers all testing requirements from all project activities and analyzes them efficient management of test resources and product test samples as well as consistency of testing philosophy.

Plans and Status

This activity creates and maintains the program anatomy, the work breakdown structure and its dictionary; gathers the performing activities' subordinate plans, coordinates (?)master scheduling, and measures and statuses program progress against these plans. Being independent of the performing activities, it provides the program an important check and balance. The disciplines and tools of this activity are discussed in Chapters 7 and 9.

Finance and Controls

Finance and controls is the keeper of the Enterprise accounting systems that gather and store the financial database of all enterprise activities, establish and maintain pricing rates, and provide the appropriate output data from the comparison of time-phased budgets and accomplishment to each level of management. The disciplines involved are discussed in Chapters 7 and 9.

4.7 "Total Quality Management" and "Continuous Improvement"

Total Quality Management (TQM) initiatives in industry and government have been a way to capture the techniques and ideas that successful organizations and projects have used to achieve their success. My company was one of those success stories. Concurrent engineering and integrated product development teams had been used in some form on well run programs for more than 35 years. Customer satisfaction was the fundamental tenet of our business. The principles of examining our practices and finding better ways of meeting program objectives had also been a characteristic of our programs, but on a careful block-change basis,--not continuously.

Our corporate response to TQM, and 6-Sigma initiatives was called CQI or Continuous Quality Improvement. The tenets of these initiatives, which are the hallmarks of success, were familiar to our organization, so I have never been comfortable with slogans, trappings, and posturing to create a new initiative for TQM. (See discussion of fads in Chapter 11). That is in no way to suggest that we didn't need to examine how we were doing our job, look for minimum-value- added activities and ways to eliminate them and do better. In fact, an Enterprise can always improve and must to remain competitive. I believe that this self-assessment is also consistent with the values of any high-integrity enterprise.

Separating Substance from Form

The end-measures of effective TQM, CQI and similar activities are results--not rhetoric. In many instances, there has been too much emphasis on process. Process is not a substitute for re-sults. It is the means to achieve the results. If results are to be achieved, then it follows that the objectives to be achieved must be specific and measurable, and the *results* measured. One of the values of dividing responsibilities organizationally is to pro-vide a point of measurement as a hand-off occurs. In teams, this relationship also exists.

One of the key tenets of TQM is the use of integrated product teams (IPTs) and concurrent engineering. Another is customer satisfaction. The approach described for implementing IPTs in this chapter is an extension of the relationships described in the previous chapters. It centers on the integrity of the people and the organizations that make up an enterprise. This philosophy is the very essence of empowerment, commitment and accounta-bility. It applies whether between individuals, between organizations, or in Integrated Product Teams. It requires mutual respect if teamwork by any name is to be real.

Integrated Product Teams Rediscovered

I led my first integrated product team in 1962. It was a project called "Lifeboat". Our job was to develop a back-up attitude control system for the early Discoverer Satellite program and to fly it within six months. In today's vernacular, the goal was to reduce cycle-time. We assembled a team co-located in a build-ing with the Discoverer Program team and they were our customer. Our team had all the ingredients of today's IPTs. We were a small group, empowered to do the job. We had representatives of all the necessary disciplines to synthesize, analyze, design, buy and build the flight and ground checkout hardware; these representatives had the full support of their home organizations.

Manufacturing technicians and planners who would build the follow-on units were part of the development team from day one. We had program representatives to establish the necessary interfaces with the Discoverer primary system. We met the challenge and the schedule.

My second experience with IPTs began in 1973 with the Trident C4 Fleet Ballistic Missile Program. Here the driver was not cycle-time, but unit production cost. These teams were called producibility teams, not IPTs. But the methodology was the same: for each segment of the system, gather representatives of all the organizations that add value to the end-item whether flight equipment, ground equipment, or software. Their job was to make everything work together -- to define the design, how it would be produced and tested, and to commit to schedule and cost for their part of the job, based on that definition. In this case, the producibility team members represented their home organizations who supported them.

The functional home organizations then implemented the plan and executed the tasks to deliver all development units, testing under operational conditions, feeding back the early results to the team for changes where needed, while simultaneously planning and tooling for production. In other words, they were using concurrent engineering. Pilot production was part of the development contract. This required proofing of the production process and maintaining the continuity of manufacture right into the initial production run, while demonstrating the actual cost, performance and reliability as built to the product disclosure data.

The project's management responsibility was to define a framework for what Peter Drucker has called "price-based costing"[5]. This framework provided for allocation and negotiation of cost targets for each segment of the product and a means for providing continuing visibility to the cost estimates as the design and producibility decisions were made. The methodology is discussed in Chapter 8.

Appendix 1 is the program management memorandum that implemented that process. Note that part of the methodology is an independent allocation of requirements, target costs, and master schedule as well as assessment of the results that gives feedback to the team on costs, first with estimated and then with actuals on early hardware.

These programs occurred long before these government quality initiatives were invented. Note that nowhere do you see a requirement for monthly progress reports on all the implementations. Our efforts were every day real activity aimed at one ultimate goal -- success measured by customer satisfaction.

These teams were motivated by one simple thing: a clear understanding of what it took to succeed. In this particular case, a well-defined multiple incentive contract provided that understanding. First, it defined the performance and interface constraints for the overall product the customer desired, and

---

[5] *Managing in a Time of Great Change* Peter F. Drucker Truly Talley Books/ Plume Press 1998

what the key attributes were worth to him. Second, it empowered the contractor to take the actions necessary to define and
deliver that product guided by incentives on performance and
cost.

Actions to provide what the customer wanted would maximize
the contractor's profit if successful and penalize falling short of
the target performance.

This type of contract is discussed in more detail in Chapter 12.
The point here is that the contractual arrangement between
buyer and seller, if it is integrity-based, causes the competent
seller to find smart and innovative approaches on their own initiative that provide customer satisfaction, if customer satisfaction
has been defined beforehand, and codified in the contract incentive value statements.

Customer Satisfaction Comes in Several Flavors

What other ways does customer satisfaction relate to making
Product Development Teams work? One approach is to invite
the ultimate customer to be part of the process as an observer,
but not as a director. When the customer is a participant and
sees how the team is dealing with its problems and resolving
them, and is part of the daily dialogue, satisfaction with the end
result is almost assured. We used to call this "kitchen privileg-
es."

If all members of the team share the same end-objective -- for
example, to develop an aircraft flight hardware segment for production -- there are still conflicting objectives about the part of
the task that each member must accomplish to meet his or her
commitments. In making those commitments, each team member is the customer of the others. This is an example of where
customer satisfaction becomes a factor internally --where initia-

tive, ownership of the task, commitment and accountability for success are demonstrated.

One counterproductive tactic is for team members to make very conservative commitments for their respective tasks. A more fruitful approach is to ask each other "What is your objective and how can I help you meet your objective while I can still meet mine?" " What kind of information do you need from me and when, to get your part of the job done?" We would use the same approach to resolve conflicts between the program and the ultimate customer on occasion.

4.8 Expectations of individuals assigned to IPTs

If you recall the seven elements of integrity in a project from Chapter 2, you have the definition of what kind of people we want to have representing each function in an integrated product team. The relationships described in Chapter 4 for a program or project also hold for IPTs, because IPTs are nothing but small projects.

I have seen IPTs succeed and I have seen them fail badly. The ones that failed did so because the members were overly impressed with their "empowerment". They were arrogant and chose to work in isolation, virtually excluding the overarching disciplines, and the expertise of their home organizations believing them to be a waste of precious resources. The chickens came home to roost -- big time! A proper IPT environment is one that functions within the framework of the organization structure, not in spite of it.

Empowerment Within Overarching System Disciplines

The empowerment of individuals and teams is consistent with our concept of integral management. But empowerment does not mean that there are no rules or constraints on the process. Nor does it mean that there are no system disciplines or constraint to an overall plan. I have seen these assumptions made with tragic results.

In order for IPTs to accomplish their objectives, it is crucial that the *integrating disciplines*, such as program planning, master scheduling, cost control, and systems engineering be represented on each team. These members are responsible to the team for determining the interfaces with other teams, as well as coordinating with the integrating functions that allocate requirements to each segment (and therefore each team) of the total system. Every team member must participate in planning and cost management for his or her activities.

Role of IPT Home Organizations and Managers.

If IPTs consist of representatives from each discipline who are empowered to speak and act for their area of expertise, then what, in the context of the organizational and managerial relationships described earlier, is the role of the home organization and its manager?

Just as checks and balances result from careful division of responsibility among organizations, that same division of responsibility on product teams helps assure that things don't get overlooked within the team. The skills and knowledge that each team member brings fulfills the functional need within the team. The hand-over to another team member at each appropriate point in the development cycle provides an objective measure of accomplishment, just as it does in functional organizational hand-offs.

The typical home organization manager will have several leaders and groups of people working on different program teams. That means that 1.) the manager must assure that each leader has available to them the necessary talent, facilities and other resources needed to meet the technical schedule and cost commitments made by their team leaders; and 2) The manager must act as a coach to each of those teams for his or her area of expertise. This includes helping to resolve bureaucratic conflicts, or helping to get bridges built with other organizations where needed.

The home organizations provide the expertise to implement the job, led by their representative on the team. Taking advantage of the home organization's participation in many projects provides a cross-flow of experience, technology and methods from those other projects.

The proper relationship of the IPT member and his/her home organization is easily understood through an analogy. Think of the product development team as a group of subcontractors working on a housing tract for a general contractor. A subcontractor will be hired to do one element of the job, such as the plumbing. Unless there are no other jobs, the owner of the plumbing company will send a foreman to the job site. The foreman will have the day-to-day responsibility for work on the site. He/she must, therefore, be a person the plumbing contractor trusts.

However, the fact that the plumbing contractor trusts the foreman and respects his or her capabilities does not mean that the plumbing contractor is going to simply forget about the foreman. The job is a commitment of the plumbing sub-contractor's company to the general contractor. For that reason, the foreman consults with and reports to his or her boss regularly, and the boss frequently visits the construction site. That way, the boss can make his or her own assessment of job progress, recommend changes, and make sure the foreman gets all the help he or she needs. That help consists of trucks and equipment, assuring that the right skills are available to the foreman on the days they are needed, creating and later ordering the bill of materials, and possibly pre-assembly of some of the hardware back at the shop. The plumbing contractor will probably have several jobs going on at once, which require varying levels of support as a function of time.

The functional organization manager in the IPT environment on a program is in the same position as the plumbing contractor performing as a subcontractor to the general contractor. The success or failure of his or her organization will be reflected in the success or failure of the IPT. Each functional manager owes it to his or her organization, and the program, to assign a capable, trusted employee to be the foreman or representative on the IPT. The people assigned to the job are a team subset, and the leadership of that subset team is delegated --by the functional manager --to his or her foreman or IPT representative. However, the manager's obligation extends further, to approve the subcontract, check regularly on the progress of the team and the functional organization's contribution to it.

4.9 Resolving Conflicts in Objectives

Because of the nature of organizational roles, conflicts can be expected from time to time. An unresolved conflict may occasionally occur between the program office and the functional organizations in the negotiation of an agreement about the cost or the performance of a job. If escalation to the program manager and the responsible major organization manager cannot resolve this conflict, it will be resolved at the general management level. It is of paramount importance to foster a team relationship, and not an adversarial relationship, in resolving problems since the end goal for all parties is presumably the same.

Note: in almost every case of a new activity, some functional manager will test the power of the program manager. If the program manager is behaving in accordance with the guidelines discussed here, it is important that he or she prevail in these conflicts. If general management is not prepared to support the program manager's position, they should privately consult with that individual to come to a win -win solution or they must replace him or her.

4.10 Summary

In this chapter, the stress has been on laying the foundation and relationships involved in high-integrity project management. Understanding these relationships provides us the background for examining the management and organization of Enterprises of various types. Later in the book we will look at the specific management disciplines required for project and enterprise success. Before doing so, however, In Chapter 5, we will examine the issues of Enterprise organization.

Chapter 5 Enterprise Management and

Organization

5.0 Introduction

This chapter will examine Enterprise management and organizational structures, the principles behind them, and the pros and cons as seen by managers, employees in the trenches, and general management.

We will look at the generic management job and some principles that can be applied to structure an effective organization and management team for several types of Enterprise. We will consider a range of models from single project Enterprises to those that may have many projects or programs going on simultaneously.

We will continue with the analogy used earlier that the Enterprise is a convoy of ships. We will use 'enterprise' non-capitalized to refer to those organizations which represent the individual ships in the convoy, or the division of effort within the Enterprise as a whole. First level or lower level managers will be defined as the leaders of these individual enterprises or ships within the whole convoy.

5.1 Two Fundamental Tests for Management Structure

We can begin this discussion with two fundamental truths to be applied, when contemplating management structure and organization:

A. <u>All managers manage some sort of enterprise having one or more customers with a charter for what they do, and five resources: people, facilities and equipment, information, money, and time.</u> *If even one of these elements is missing, the organization should not exist!* (Note: by time I mean that if the need for the function is much less than one year, the function should probably be fulfilled by a task force or other *ad hoc* approach using existing organizations.)

B. <u>Higher level managers supervise managers to whom they have delegated authority within their Enterprise, providing guidance and resolving conflicts among them.</u> *If higher-level managers do not meet this definition, <u>they</u> should not exist!*

5.2 Organizing for Success

There are many ways to organize and manage an Enterprise to accomplish a mission. Most effective organizations seem to share some common characteristics. When they lose these characteristics, they lose the magic. So how should you as a leader organize your enterprise to best accomplish your mission?

The Importance of Organizational Clarity

A table of organization or organization chart should define an Enterprise's delegation of its mission with clarity (unless you want to hide some activity). Organizations are not blocks on a wiring diagram, but are groups of people with hopes, fears, pride, prejudices, strengths and weaknesses. Again, the convoy analogy seems appropriate.

Cargo ships, oilers, and combat ships have their captains, crews, and a part of the overall mission. It is important that each part know how it relates to the whole. How they are segmented, how they are managed, and how they relate to each other has a profound effect on how they perceive the Enterprise and how well they perform within it. The thoughtful creation of the organization chart is a key communication of intended behavior.

Working at different levels in many types of organizations over 40 years offered me the opportunity to encounter and see the strengths and weaknesses of many approaches to management and organization as Enterprises grew and I grew with them. Here I will examine various viewpoints in the typical Enterprise, each with its own set of hopes, fears, triumphs and frustrations.

Five Guiding Principles for Organization Structure Integrity

These principles spring from the fundamentals that we discussed in Section 5.1. If followed, they should facilitate accomplishment of the mission of any Enterprise by making the jobs of individual managers and those who report to them easier and clearer at all levels of the Enterprise.

The five principles:

1) The organizational partitioning should provide for *a clear division and delegation of responsibility and authority* with a clear understanding of the bounds of that delegation, without stifling innovation and the application of common sense.

2) The organization partitioning should be compatible with *contracting integrity* among the parts with objectives that incentivize a team approach to meet the Enterprise mission, and with the provision of checks and balances to help identify problems. Contracting integrity means having the ability to commit, and control over what it takes to meet that commitment. (See Fundamental Truth A earlier in this chapter)

3) The organization structure should *recognize the value of all disciplines* and specialties as well as the *checks and balances* needed to successfully fulfill the mission.

4) The organization structure should *minimize duplication of common disciplines, tools, and processes* without undermining the delegations of principle 1 and without creating a conflict of interest for any manager or employee.

5) The organization should *allow flexibility* to grow, adapt to change, and fix problems without major disruption or losing the strengths of the enterprise;

5.3 Roles and missions defined by titles and charters communicate the intended division of responsibility within the Enterprise

An important test of an organization structure is to draw the chart with the organization names and wiring diagram, and then to write bullets under each box that delineate that organization's responsibilities as defined in its charter. If you find more than one organization with any of the same bullets, you should ask why. If no one can explain why in terms of the five organizational principles, then you have failed the test of organizational clarity. Figure 5-1 shows an example of this technique.

Ambiguity causes unnecessary and unproductive conflict.

A close look at the example of Figure 5-1 will show potential overlap between functions identified as marketing and functions in technical support. There is also potential overlap between product returns in marketing and stores under operations. Often it matters less where a function resides than that it resides in just one place. I have seen all sorts of conflict caused by the simple failure to clarify roles and missions. That energy should be applied to the mission of the Enterprise.

Organizational Conflict Check

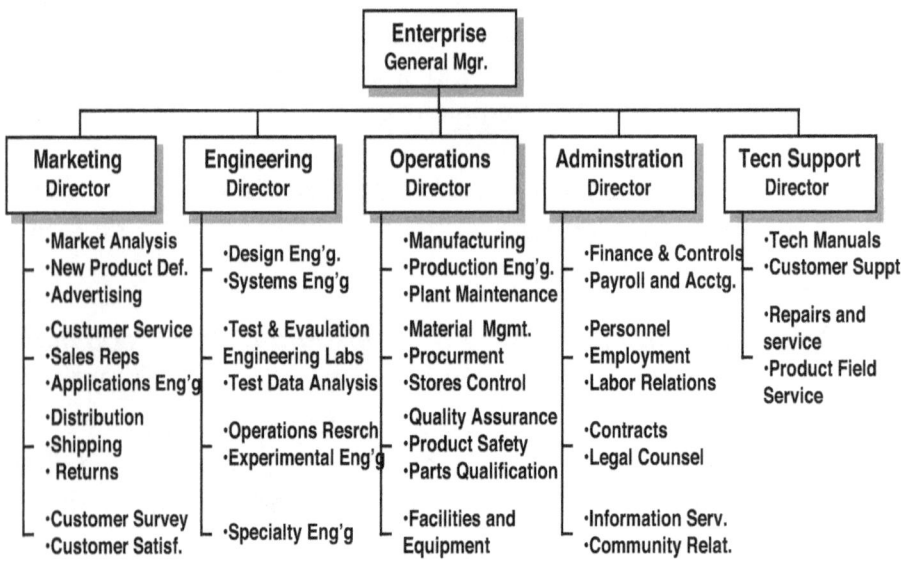

Figure 5-1 Organization Conflict Test

Competition vs. Conflict

Sometimes it is desirable to create competitive activities in order to achieve a greater goal. If so, get the competition on the table openly and be prepared to deal with its fruits. An example of a desirable competition would be two potential solutions to a critical problem pursued separately in parallel.

Setting Expectations

Define the contract with every organization. Measures of performance are part of the contract -- expectations, constraints, standards, and how you expect to be kept informed.

5.4 Organization Models

Now we are ready to think about the form of our Enterprise organization. Where is the Enterprise in its evolution? We will look at four evolutionary states and apply the principles of Section 5.2 to suggest effective tables of organization, considering the viewpoints of the managers within that construct and the potential for conflicting objectives among them.

The Small, Single-product Enterprise

This one (schematically shown in figure 5-2) is the easiest to think about and the simplest to implement. It is how most new start-ups begin.

When there is only one product, everyone is working on that product all the time, in effect. All resources are directed to that product. There is no one working who is not paid for by the revenues of that product, no matter what they are working on. Therefore, the project manager for that product owns everything in the enterprise, and may even be the head of the company.

Suppose we apply the tests of the five principles of section 5.2 to this model by asking the following questions:

- What are the disciplines required and how much for how long? (Make vs. buy strategy/decisions determine how many people are needed, but not the need to have that discipline represented in-house.)

- Which of these disciplines have common heritages, talent pools, education and experience? (Can one manager effectively take on more than one?)

Organization Example
Single Product Enterprise

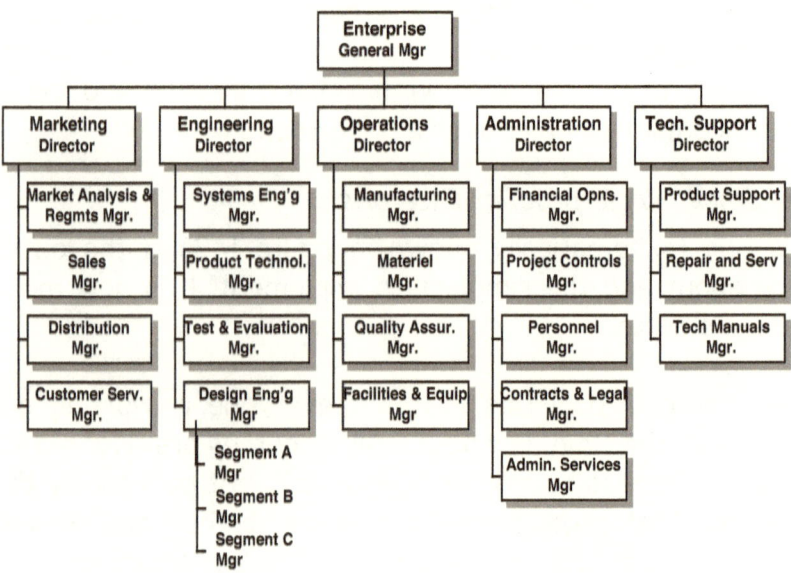

Figure 5-2 Single- project Enterprise

The answer to these two questions establishes the lowest level of leadership responsibility. In this example, there are three sub-systems or segments in the product with different characteristics.

- Which disciplines are fundamentally embedded in the enterprise and cannot therefore be purchased outside? This gets to the issue of value added and vulnerability to loss of control.

- What portions of the work required should be done in-house and what parts are better done by outside suppliers, and why? This determines what size various organizations should be.

- What checks and balances are needed
    a) to meet the fiduciary responsibilities to customers, suppliers, investors, or regulatory agencies (independent financial audit and reporting)?
    b) to provide self-governance within the enterprise. For example, test and evaluation and quality assurance functions that are independent of design or software coding, contract and subcontract administration?
    c) to provide different viewpoints (marketing, customer relations)

The answer to these questions defines functions <u>that must be on a comparable level</u> to the much larger development and manufacturing functions.

The medium to large multi-product Enterprise with one customer segment and common disciplines among the products.

Figure 5-3 shows a schematic of this type of Enterprise
- The same disciplines are required, but they must be working on three projects at the same time. The projects are probably in different stages of development so the functional disciplines will be required for an extended time.

- The same make vs. buy strategy/decisions are assumed to apply, but suppliers may be different on each project, requiring a larger procurement function.
- The disciplines have common heritages, talent pools, education and experience, so the same management structure exists, but again on a larger scale.

Organization Example
MediumSize Single Customer Base Multi- Product Enterprise

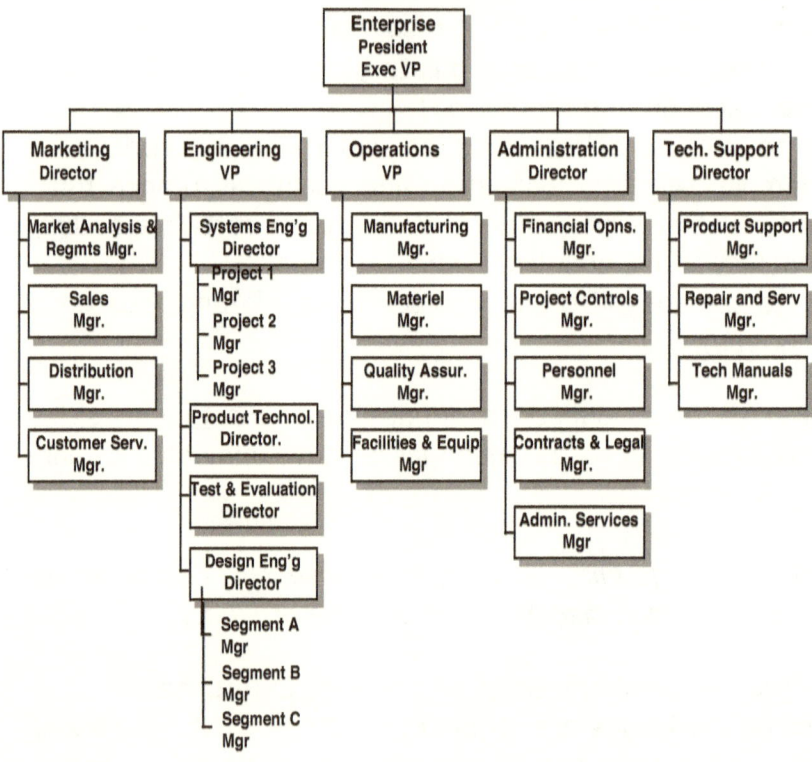

Figure 5-3

- The disciplines are fundamentally embedded in the enterprise and cannot therefore be purchased outside.

- Because there are three projects underway serving the same customer base, the customer interface hasn't changed.

However there is now a need for some dedicated project leadership in the product design area, as shown.

- Since the products in the example involve the same disciplines, I have assumed that the same portions of the work required should be done in-house.

- The checks and balances are the same.

The medium-to-large multi-product Enterprise with many customers and common disciplines among the products

Figure 5-4 illustrates an example of this Enterprise model. I have assumed that the disciplines required for the products this Enterprise makes are the same as in the previous examples. Since we are talking about the same kinds of products, I have assumed the same make vs. buy strategy/decisions; however, this is not inherent in the model. Capacity limits might dictate more buy, or the business base might be large enough to justify investment in in-house capability for some items previously purchased.

We still have the same disciplines with common heritages, talent pools, education and experience. Now with a multiple product base and many customers, it is no longer possible for the Enterprise President and the Marketing Organization to be the primary interface with all customers. In this model, at least three of the products or projects are now big enough to warrant a full-time management function.

Some issues and observations about this type of organization are listed below:
- Should product management be divided by type of product, by customer, by geography or by some other factor?

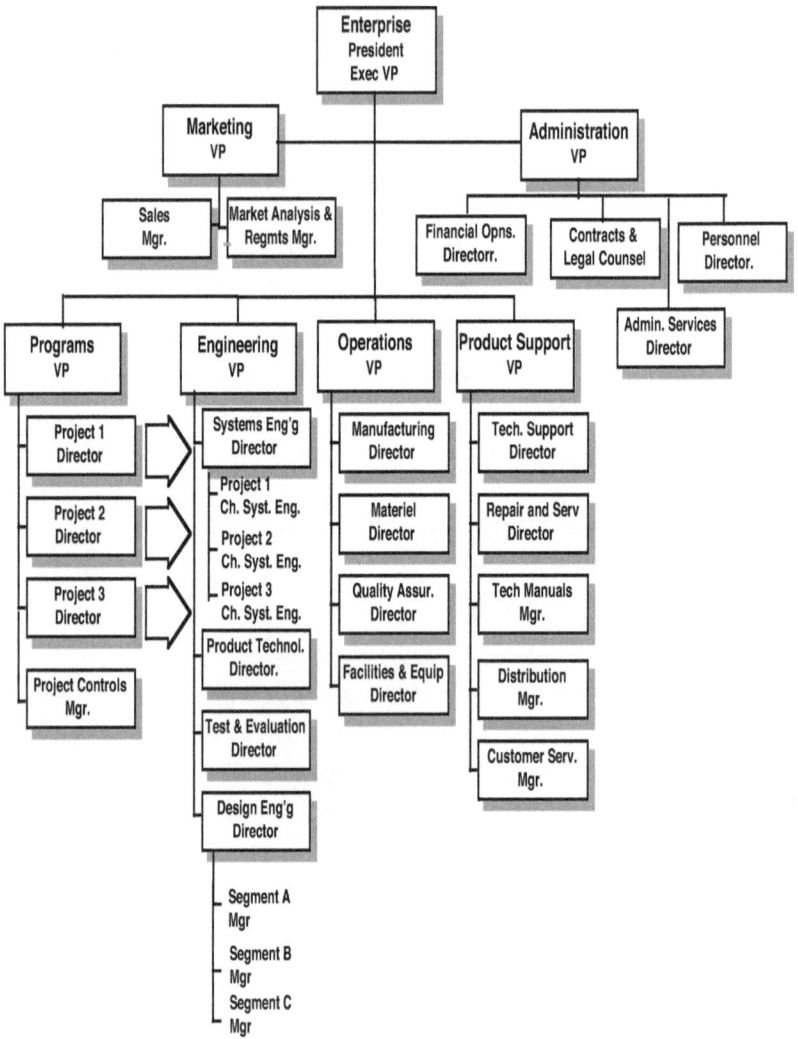

Organization Example
Multiple Customer Base Multi- Product Enterprise

Figure 5-4

- Which disciplines are fundamentally embedded in the enterprise and cannot therefore be purchased outside? Competitive teaming may determine what portions of the work required should be done in house and what parts are better done by teammates or suppliers.

- With many projects or products, there may be longevity and breadth enough to projectize certain disciplines in stable, dedicated organizations without duplicating effort. However, in this example I have shown project management offices that integrate across the functional organizations for their projects as denoted by the three arrow symbols. This example is approximately the model for the organization and management relationships discussed in the previous chapter.

- Note the titles in the various organization boxes on the chart. If comparable levels don't exist between project management and functional management, this type of organization fails. Perception is important to the Enterprise, which takes cues from titles and relative levels. In order not to create a very busy chart I have not shown lower reporting structure, but it is assumed that all director-level positions have at least one level of management reporting to them.

- Note also that the Enterprise has grown sufficiently to have a VP of administration with program controls no longer reporting to that box. There is now a chief legal counsel. The Enterprise also has enough product activity to warrant moving some of the service functions from marketing over to what is now called product support. Marketing now concentrates on sales to new customers, while the projects with product support for service take care of existing customers.

- The same checks and balances are needed, but perhaps the enterprise has gone public and has new requirements.

Figure 5-5 diagrams this heavily projectized example. The projects are now large enough and long enough in duration to be called programs.

The medium to large sized multi-product Enterprise with many customers and unique disciplines for each product or group of products

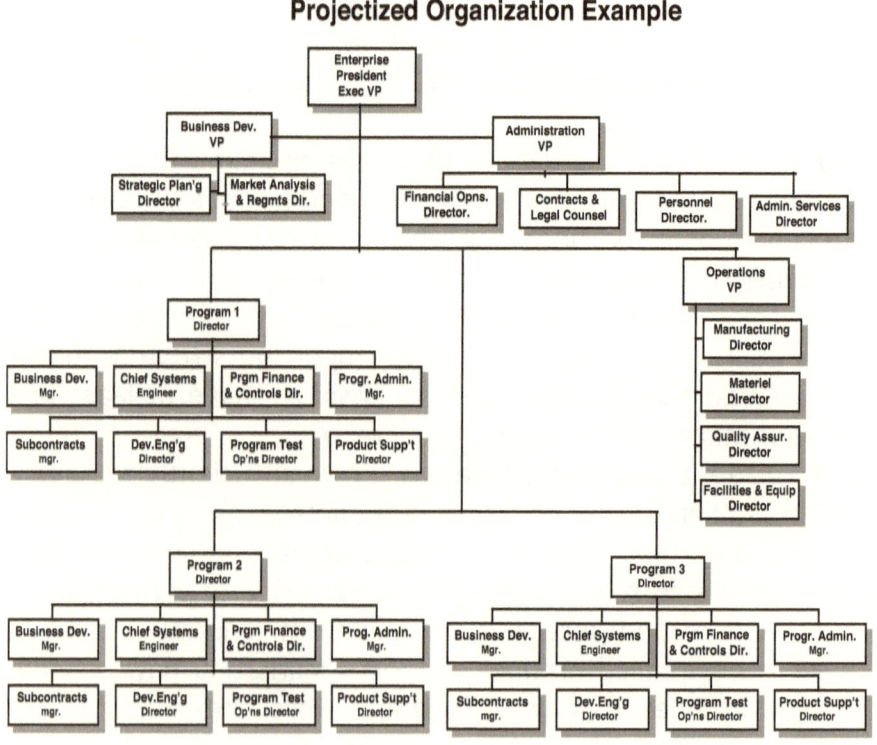

Figure 5-5

Only two management levels are shown for simplicity, but the substructures are similar to earlier examples. Some of the disciplines required are unique to each program or product line, so the Enterprise has projectized many functions. You can see that one effect of projectization is a duplication of functions within the Enterprise. In this case, only manufacturing and administrative functions remain centralized. In the case of manufacturing it is because of the large investments in facilities and equipment involved. Enterprise administrative functions still report direct to the president's office for fiduciary reasons, but program-related finance and control functions have been delegated to the programs. The Marketing and Business Development functions have largely been assigned to the programs, while the Enterprise function has become more oriented to new markets and strategic planning for new endeavors.

Combinations of the above.

Of course, there are many combinations of the above examples and many totally different structures that can be constructed. Most will work if they satisfy the principles outlined earlier in this chapter, and have the relationships discussed in Chapter 4. Conversely, there is no organization structure that will work if these principles are violated.

5.5 Projectized vs. Matrix Organizations

Over the years much has been made of organizing by project versus organizing by a matrix of function and project.

- In the case-model of section 5.4.1 there is no issue. It's all projectized by definition. In section 5.4.2, there is only one customer base, there are several products at the same location that are competing for resources and facilities, and if each is fully projectized, by definition we are facing duplication at many levels. I chose in the example to create project engineers to integrate the design of each product within the Enterprise. Section 5.4.3 introduces the concept of program or project offices that are dedicated to the management and integration of all activities required to accomplish that project.

- Finally, the next section introduces a heavily projectized organization driven by three things: disparate customer bases, unique engineering disciplines, and unique test facilities. But it is also clear that this model necessitates duplication of management talent across the board, and duplication of other resources as well. When does this make sense and when does it not?

Arguments For and Against Projectization

When discussing new programs, the question of projectization arises quickly and often heatedly. It is suggested that the program manager can exert greater control if all relevant program personnel, including engineering and operations personnel, are on the program's "badge". It is alleged that only then will the program manager have the requisite level of commitment from all the people working on his program.

If you ask almost any program manager about this, they will attest, for example, that when they don't have to depend on the cooperation of other organizations to meet their objectives, they don't have to expend enormous energy negotiating with their peer managers. If negotiations become stalled, as they often will, and the program manager has to go to general management for resolution, his power is eroded. Moreover, if organizational leadership on either side is allowed to engage in game-playing, the program manager's job becomes impossible. If all the resources report to the program organization, these issues are eliminated.

There are also problems with projectization, however. As you might expect, the fully projectized organization managers in a multi-project enterprise end up in conflict with other projects vying for priority in resources and facilities. And the checks and balances of the aforementioned negotiations, while they may be time-consuming, can prevent serious mistakes of lack of experience in areas of the job.

In fact, the distinction between projectization and the matrix is not as clear-cut as one might think. I suggest that excepting an organization with only one project, there has never been a purely projectized organization. Any project that had every support person badged to its organization would be unwieldy and inefficient. Projectization and use of the matrix exist in all projects -- the only distinction is in the proportions of each. <u>The success of these activities depends on the integrity of the involved management in fulfilling their respective roles.</u> These roles are discussed in detail in Chapter 4. Interestingly enough, the more experienced project managers become, the less concerned they tend to be about who is badged where, if general management is doing its job in maintaining integrity.

My Preferred Model

If we think of a program as a task force, with every member of the task force committed to the program, then the question of to whose badge or organization the people report is irrelevant. All that remains is to establish conditions that make commitments among the organizations involved real and binding. The first of these conditions is empowerment. Representatives of functional organizations, co-located with the program, have the power to speak and make commitments on behalf of their functional organizations.   Day-to-day decision-making authority should never reside with a remote "home organization". Additionally, there should be one person with authority at each "intersection" in the matrix -- not one from the program and one from the functional organization.

Organization Example
Multiple project Matrix Structure

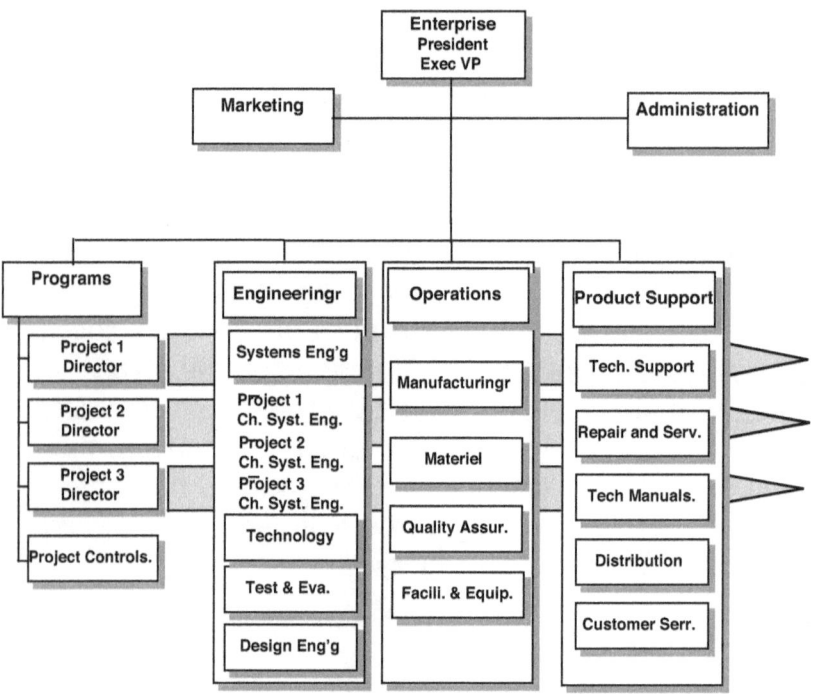

Figure 5-6

Figure 5-6 illustrates my preferred model. I submit that in a company that has multiple projects or programs in progress, the most efficient approach is a hybrid organization which uses functional organizations to provide the expertise to many projects, while some functions are projectized. The gray horizontal arrows cutting across functional organizations depict the program integration and coordination job of the program or project management teams, and the relationships described in Chapter 4.

Chapter 4 presented in a project context my view of the management relationships and guidelines that engender success. They have been very successful in a predominantly "matrix" organization structure, with centralized functional organizations serving all programs.

In my experience, the matrix organization structure was the toughest crucible for management relationships. High-integrity relationships were expected, and these organizations functioned well. Certainly there were conflicts, but they were settled constructively and quickly. *It is up to general management to set the guidelines and the environment for successful implementation of a matrix structure, and to recognize when lubrication is needed to keep the system running smoothly.*

The guidelines of Chapter 4 build and depend on high-integrity relations between all the parties, and setting and maintaining that environment is the most important responsibility of general management. This means specifically that *general management must clearly demonstrate by action what behavior is rewarded and tolerated.* As we know, actions speak volumes more than the noblest words. Failure of general management to act congruently with its words undermines all trust. I hope the reader can now start to see how this fabric of integrity is woven through every facet of our Enterprise.

5.6 Some Other Organizational Issues

Acquiring and Maximizing the Utilization of Key Talent

Examine the disciplines needed to support the product lines of the Enterprise. Organize to establish responsibility for the acquisition and effectiveness of those disciplines. This is one argument for not projectizing commonly used disciplines. Having a centralized function allows the cross flow of experience, technology and methods from one project to another.

Implications of Make-or-Buy Decisions on Organization

The decision to buy instead of making a segment of a product does not affect the need for in-house activities (other than manufacturing); only the size of the staffing required to implement the work. One of the frequent mistakes made is to make a decision to buy from a supplier without establishing a qualified buying expertise. This almost always leads to trouble.

Spans of Control, Deputies, and Assistants. "Flat" Organizations

Periodically, someone gets all worked up about so-called measures of management efficiency, such as span of control -- the number of people reporting to a given level of management. A popular "right" number is seven. More is "better" because it "flattens" the organization. Eliminating levels of management is also a popular theme. Another popular belief is that there should not be deputy or assistant managers. I suggest that these ideas are hogwash! Remember "Pretty Good Rule #2"? First of all, the "right" span of control, and the need for a deputy or assistant, is a function of workload and time away from the office, not some arbitrary number; and believe me, the workload is very different for different organizations. I have flattened organizations, recognizing the risks, but not using those criteria.

It is also currently popular to talk about "Best Practices". I have noticed that most of the people talking about them have at least two difficulties. One is discerning the differences between apples and oranges: they assume that what has succeeded in one situation will also succeed in another. The second is applying what they espouse to themselves. I always shudder as the "best practices" staffs start staffing up so that they can gather metrics to reduce the number of people working elsewhere.

Careful benchmarking of peer organizations and Enterprises is a good thing as long as one understands all the differences in the nature of things being compared.   I believe that the most valid and enduring measures of "lean-ness" are supervisory and managerial ratios over a large sector of the Enterprise, without trying to jam every organization into a standard mold. Supervisory ratio is simply the average total number of employees per supervisory personnel (including all managers). In my business, a supervisory ratio of about 7 to 1 seemed to be right for the Enterprise as a whole. But some organizations belonged at 40 to 1, while others might quite logically be 1 to1. Similarly, the average number of employees per manager was about 35 to 1, but some organizations could be more than 200 to 1 while others were 2 or 3 to 1.

I personally don't believe in more than one deputy or assistant, unless they are deputies *for* some management function. The usual place for these is in project offices where, because they are management organizations, the total staff is purposely small, and the management job is across the entire Enterprise as illustrated in figure 5-6. My observation is that assistants or deputies to higher-level managers fulfill two important objectives. One is to maintain decision continuity in high throughput environments, while one or the other is on travel, or otherwise away from the office, and where an acting subordinate cannot effectively make the decisions. Second, it provides a valuable training and testing opportunity for the deputy for succession planning.

On the other hand, in large functional organizations with lots of subordinate supervisory or management structure, it is desirable to try to let subordinate managers act for their next level up in order to train and test their skills for advancement. Typically, these types of organizations have a more orderly environment over time, so that the risk of a mistake is lower than in a program management environment. But again, it depends on the situation. One critical job may already have a ready backup available, where another may need to develop one.

My point is simply that benchmarking by comparing large peer Enterprises with similar markets makes sense, but it is wrong to try to fit all levels and all parts with the same suit. There are no universal hard and fast rules.

Overarching disciplines and their delegation

Overarching disciplines are the subject of Chapter 7, and are sometimes overlooked in the interest of saving money. This generally turns out to be penny- wise and pound foolish. In this chapter we examined organizational structures where these functions were delegated from the project manager to one or more functional organizations. This will work fine, as long as the delegate is given the charter and authority to enforce it. For product disciplines such as systems engineering or product safety, the clout required can be enforced by the design review process and the technical performance assessment mechanisms.

Division of Responsibility: Key Checks & Balance.

Division of responsibility provides important checks and balances in the conduct of operations within an Enterprise of any size. In each of the examples we looked at in section 5.7, the last test was about Enterprise checks and balances. Similarly, in the development and production process, divisions of responsibility that require hand off to a separate group for evaluation have some benefits. Handoff of the product design when deemed ready to a separate organization with the skills and knowledge for independent evaluation and hand-over of manufactured product or software programs to quality assurance for acceptance does the same thing.   First, it gets emotional investment in creation off the table during evaluation, and second, the hand-over provides a definitive measurement point of accomplishment and the quality of that accomplishment.

Centralized vs. Distributed Support Functions

Finally, an observation about support functions and how they are handled. By support functions, I mean administrative and personnel support; and business management functions such as procurement, financial budgeting and control, strategic planning and marketing. Much heat and little light have been generated on the subject of how support functions should be organized. While centralizing support functions appeals to the bean counters, claiming efficiency, it tends to turn the function from an enabling function to a thwarting function, and the importance of this should not be minimized.

My feeling is that support means helping and understanding, and that means proximity and local control. So, except for those things that must be centralized for the integrity of the Enterprise, such as financial accounting systems and facility acquisition and utilization, support functions should be distributed with only small central staff coordination groups to keep the Enterprise integrated.

Chapter 6 Subcontract Management

6.0 Introduction

This chapter describes management roles and responsibilities for subcontract management and integration. The guidelines presented here have been widely used in the most successful programs. The purpose of this chapter is to reinforce these practices as a model for integral management of subcontracts.

6.1 Background

As discussed earlier, when our model enterprise commits to develop and deliver a major product, it assigns a program manager to act as the customer's agent to the company and the company's agent to the customer. The purpose is to assure that: 1) an equitable business relationship is established in a contract that defines the work to be done; (2) a mutually agreed-to cost is established for the conduct of the effort; and (3) the necessary resources are brought to bear to accomplish the work in accordance with the contract. If the project is a new product funded within the company, the customer is general management, but the duties are the same.

The program manager acts like a general contractor "subcontracting" the work, other than program requirements and integration, to entities that are skilled in the necessary disciplines to best perform the work required. In our model those "subcontractors" are the functional branches. I have used the terms *subcontracting and subcontractor* in quotes to connote a conceptual relationship between a project or program manager within the Enterprise acting as the general contractor, and functional organizations within the Enterprise who take on the role of "subcontractor" for some portion of the work. These relationships within the Enterprise should be no different whether the work is "subcontracted" within the Enterprise or subcontracted to an outside supplier.

In both cases we are seeking a partnership for the long term with the same needs for contractual definition, integration with the other ongoing activities, checks and balances, and status and controls. Chapter 4 described relationships that should be in place for "contracting" within the enterprise. This chapter addresses supplier relationships and the checks and balances within the Enterprise to assure integrity in those relationships.

Typically, half of the total contracted work in a complex project is procured from sources outside of the Enterprise. Subcontract management and integration is therefore an extremely important part of the activity. The subcontract management concept described here emphasizes the close coordination of several functional organizations, each responsible for defining parts of what any given subcontractor will do. The challenge is to integrate these requirements to be consistent with the strategy, goals and requirements of the overall program.

6.2 Make or Buy Decisions

In the formulation of a program strategy, the program or project manager should prepare the proposed make or buy plan with the participation of supporting organizations. This plan should be formulated and approved before any bids are solicited from outside suppliers. If a decision is made to solicit supplier bids for a portion of the work, there should be no competition except by other suppliers. That is to say, because of the potential for conflict of interest, no part of the Enterprise should be allowed to compete with outside suppliers bidding for the work. The only circumstances in which I would modify that philosophy are: 1) in the event that a supplier competitively selected either failed to perform the work; 2) if in the bid instructions, it was clearly identified that there was a *make and* buy decision, in which case the supplier would legitimately limit the information he would provide to the prime prior to the final decision; or 3) there was a pre-agreed commitment to dual-sourcing with an up-front definition of the split.

6.3 Source Selection

In selecting sources of supply for any commodity or service, we seek a competent reliable supplier with a good competitively priced product solution, who is interested in being a valued member of the project team, and who shares the buyer's values. Usually this objective is best achieved by comparative shopping in a way that allows the buyer to make an accurate judgement based on these criteria. Sometimes, the choice is obvious, and should be made outright using negotiations to assure an equitable fit. But usually, particularly in the case of a new requirement, the most effective approach is to conduct a competition.

A buyer with integrity will never hold a competition when he or she already knows who will win. Most complaints about procurement selections arise because someone felt misled. It should be assumed that regardless of the selection method used, someone will be unhappy and will seek to protest. Therefore, unambiguous descriptions of the basis to be used for selection, and rigorous evaluations with thorough documentation are a must, and will save lots of grief later.

Competition and its Value

Competition is a method for dealing with a management problem. It should be used judiciously, but it is frequently misused.

The acquisition of commodities, products, or services, presents four common types of problem that can be alleviated by competition. The first is when the buyer is not sure what to buy. Here the objectives are to see what alternatives are available to address the need, and then to pick the best solution and competency at an acceptable cost for that solution. The type of contract envisioned has a big influence on the criteria for selection. For instance, if you want some or all rights to the solution, you have to pay for it. There will be changes as you and the supplier define the requirements and solution, so the cost of doing business is more important than a bid price. See Chapter 12 for more on contract types.

The second problem is when the buyer knows exactly what to buy, but doesn't know what it should cost. Here the assumption is that any qualified bidder's product is technically acceptable and we are seeking the lowest price offering. This is simple enough, but the difficulty is in knowing that the first assumption is correct. In any case, if a competition is conducted fairly, the buyer must be willing to accept any of the bidders based on the selection criteria defined for the competition. If the assumption doesn't hold, the buyer should restrict the bidders to those who can satisfy that requirement. It is a waste of all parties' time and money to do otherwise.

The third is when the buyer needs to maintain several sources of supply at least through some point to reduce risk of failure. Multiple sourcing to a down-select point is also a good way to prevent a "buy-in:" a low initial bid designed to eliminate the competition with the intent to get well in the follow-on business. Here again, contract forms are important and it is appropriate to tell the bidders what it takes to win at the time of down select or selection of a single supplier down the road.

The fourth problem is when the buyer is dissatisfied with the commitment or performance of a current supplier and unable to achieve an improvement in that performance. In other words, that supplier is no longer holding up his or her end of the team relationship.

Screening out unqualified bidders can be accomplished by sending out requests for information (RFI's) to any interested parties with the objectives of the procurement and necessary qualifications. The responses to those requests together with site visits usually filter out the ne'er-do-wells. It is not unusual, however, to have some competitor you have disqualified demand to have a chance to bid the job, and this can create a dilemma if the RFI was not carefully composed. If that job was done properly and the responses fairly evaluated and documented, a meeting with the offended supplier generally suffices to end it. If not, be ready for a protest to some higher authority. Any good buyer will tell you that comes with the territory.

Selected Source vs. Competitive Acquisition

As we said, if you already know who you are going to select, don't go through a sham competition. Be courageous. The RFI process is a good way to shake the tree without you or other suppliers wasting a lot of money. Some excellent and lasting supplier selections have been made outright on the basis of a face-to-face discussion. While some government agencies prime contracts require all subcontracts to be competitive, it is usually possible using evidence from RFI's to convince them that there is no justification in conducting the competition.

Re-competing On-going Work

Unless you are buying nails and don't care what kind you get, or your current supplier has failed to live up to commitments, re-competing for production or follow on production just to drive cost down is a really bad idea. The cost to properly qualify another source to meet the need generally exceeds any perceived savings. So when you are angry and ready to take that step, count to ten and think it through. The government sometimes competes production as a standard policy, at a tremendous and unjustified cost. Consider the effect on a supplier if he knows regardless of how well he does in meeting your need, you are going to re-compete him in production. Is that contractor likely to be completely open with you? Is he going to take the long-term team view in decisions affecting the project? Not likely.

There are a few exceptions. When you must maintain or establish more than one source of supply to avoid risk, or achieve more production capacity, you have already committed to the cost of qualifying the multiple sources' products and are using all of them successfully. Ammunition might be a good example.

6.4 Program Subcontract Integration and Management

Since a major project typically involves significant content that must be acquired from sources outside of the Enterprise, it is incumbent on the Enterprise to pay careful attention to the management of that effort. Accordingly, the Subcontract management approach suggested here is intended to emphasize (1) clear commitments to excellence in performance; (2) measurement of performance; (3) internal Enterprise "ownership" and pride in the subcontracted product; and (4) integrity on the part of all individuals and groups, both company and subcontractor, who are working on the product. This includes all aspects of the project whether technical, quality, schedule, or cost performance. "Ownership" includes two elements:

1) The acceptance of responsibility by an Enterprise individual for the performance of all effort for which budget responsibility has been delegated.

2) The acceptance of responsibility for and pride in the end-item performance in its intended usage even when others have been delegated the downstream budget responsibility. This includes the performance of equipment, software or data in its ultimate use, whether it is a test or operational application.

3) Program Office as the program requirements and integration representative;

4) Program Status/Controls where warranted. Other functional representatives from Test Engineering, Manufacturing, and quality requirements and evaluation representative; or other areas may be required and included in the team depending on the subcontract and its current status.

6.5 Subcontract Management Team and its Tasks

The idea here is basically to establish an Integrated Product Team for each major subcontract that is planned. Chairmanship of the subcontract management team will change as the subcontract effort matures from design to production. During the prime contract and subcontract proposal and negotiation phases the Program Office representative may be the chairperson. The subsystem manager's delegate will normally act as the chairperson from start of design through production design freeze. The Materiel subcontract representative will usually fill the position of chairperson from production design freeze through the completion and closure of the subcontract.

The precise timing of the change of chairperson will depend on the subcontract involved and the specific circumstances at the time of change. It must be recognized that there will probably be transition phases rather than precise transfer dates.

A. Developing the Subcontract Procurement Package

One of the initial functions of the subcontract management team is the development of a subcontract procurement package. The task of preparing this package and accomplishing all of the intermediate steps leading to the award of the subcontract requires the combined efforts of individuals representing the various functional organizations.

This procurement package must provide

- Subcontract definition based on and accurately reflecting all of the applicable prime contract requirements.

- Key events pertaining to subcontractor efforts in support of the in-house program master schedule. These milestones will start from the end-item delivery date that will support the overall program, working backward using executable spans, based on experience, to the start of subcontractor production. Compatible in-house milestones will also be established starting with subcontract placement, working backward through negotiation and receipt of contractor proposals to subcontractor task definition.

- Technical, schedule, hardware, software and data delivery requirements, acceptance criteria as well as business, programmatic and other requirements for each of the applicable functional disciplines.

- The method of selection and the criteria that will be the basis of selection of the successful subcontractor, as well as the contract form anticipated.

(The expertise to integrate and coordinate the functional inputs with the prime contract requirements and goals and the program schedule, programmatic and budgetary constraints normally will be in the Program Office. Therefore, the Program Office representative will normally chair the team during this period.)

B. Subcontractor Selection

The team conducts the source selection process following applicable policies and procedures, and prepares the results for review and approval by the designated source selection authority within the Enterprise.

C. Implementing the Subcontract Effort

The team negotiates the subcontract if required and, prior to award, assures that it is consistent with the prime contract negotiated requirements and resources.

(As part of the checks and balances to ensure acquisition integrity, the functional authority and expertise for the processes in B) and C) are in the Materiel and Subcontracts organization. Therefore, the Materiel subcontract representative to the team normally should chair the team during these periods.)

D. Evaluating Subcontractor Performance

The team attends design reviews, which will be chaired by the subsystem manager's delegate to the team. At least monthly, the team also monitors the subcontractor's technical, schedule and cost performance against plans and requirements. The team will coordinate workarounds, recovery schedules, changes, etc., and assure compatibility with the balance of the program effort.

If the commodity is an off the shelf item requiring no development effort, this effort is curtailed to monitoring delivery commitments to assure they will be met.

The functional expertise in these areas will reside with the sub-system manager's delegate, who will therefore normally chair the team during this period supported by the procurement representative and others as needed.

6.6 Functions and Responsibilities

Each functional representative on the subcontract management team is his or her organization's spokesperson for that subcontract, including that organization's "ownership" responsibilities during all phases of the procurement. As a team partner, each member is expected to provide the technical and management excellence of their parent functional organization necessary to assure that the subcontract achieves the results committed to by their functional organization. Each team member will also be responsible for monitoring and controlling the budget allocated to his or her functional organization for managing their subcontract, and will share with all of the team members the responsibility for adherence to the overall subcontract technical, cost and schedule performance of the subcontract.

Each team member, along with his or her functional manager, is expected to assume this "ownership" attitude toward the segment of the product that they have committed to provide. They are also charged with accomplishing their organization's commitments for the subsystem or equipment as a whole. These objectives require each team member to establish effective relationships and work in concert with the other functional team members to assure that all interdependent program tasks are completed successfully.

In addition to these common responsibilities, each team member has specific functions and responsibilities, including those described below:

Subsystem manager

In the case of a subsystem or equipment that is procured from an outside source, the subsystem manager is responsible for the technical direction of subcontracting activities needed to secure the development and production of items for which he or she is responsible. In carrying out this technical responsibility, the subsystem manager shares with other contributing functional organization managers the responsibility for maintaining schedule and adhering to planned cost constraints.

Subsystem manager's delegate - The Responsible Equipment Engineer:

This individual, generally from engineering, is the team technical leader and as such is responsible for and cognizant over all technical requirements of the subcontract. Within the constraints of the subcontract, he or she provides technical direction to the subcontractor, monitors the subcontractor's technical performance, chairs design reviews, dispositions design departures, monitors and controls budget allocated to engineering for the subcontract, and shares with other team members the responsibility for maintaining schedule and adhering to planned cost constraints.

Subcontract administrator and team business manager

The Materiel subcontract representative is the team's contracting officer and as such is the expert on the "rules of the road" for procurement. He or she is also the responsible for evaluating subcontractor cost and schedule performance and accomplishment against subcontract requirements. The Subcontract administrator will chair all subcontract negotiations, participate in prime contract negotiations on subcontract matters, coordinate within the team and provide all contractual direction to the subcontractor, receive and distribute all subcontract reports, data and correspondence, monitor and control the budget allocated to the Materiel organization for the subcontract, share with other team members the responsibility for maintaining schedule and adhering to planned cost constraints, function as the team business manager and provide program and general management with periodic team status reports.

Product or Quality Assurance representative

The Product Assurance representative is the team quality manager and as such is responsible for developing the subcontract quality requirements for the procurement specifications and assuring that they are consistent with the prime contract quality requirements. He or she also participates in failure analysis and quality direction to the subcontractor, and monitors and controls budget allocated to Product Assurance for the subcontract and shares with other team members the responsibility for maintaining schedule and adhering to planned cost constraints.

Program Office representative

The Program Office representative provides program requirements and coordinates their incorporation into the subcontract, monitors the integration of the team members' functional effort, tracks subcontracts progress against the program plan, helps develop contingency plans as necessary, and monitors overall cost performance. The form of subcontract to be used should be determined in the same way as are Enterprise contracts with its customers. These concepts are discussed in detail in chapter 12.

Chapter 7 Integration Arts

7.0. The Overarching Disciplines

To establish and maintain an integrated and successful implementation of a project or program, requires some specific disciplines, first to get everyone on the same page, and then keep them together as the project progresses. These disciplines which are critical, but often not appreciated by the participants, can be described as follows: 1) *program* definition and integration; 2) *program* evaluation; 3) *product* definition and integration; and 4) *product* evaluation. I will describe what I mean by each of these, and then look at the methods for assuring their effective implementation, including communication media, processes, tools, and data interpretation.

7.1 Program Definition and Integration

In Chapter 3, we discussed the program plan as the basic foundation of program definition and implementation, and also discussed the planning process. Chapter 4 described the management and organizational relationships involved. Here, we are concerned with implementing that plan, keeping it coordinated, and tracking progress with respect to it.

If the plan is to be implemented well, it must be defined in sufficient detail that responsibilities and expectations are clear.

The Statement of work

The requirements and objectives of any project are invoked in a statement of work. Whether the project is a contracted activity for a customer outside the Enterprise, or funded by the Enterprise, some description of the work to be done must be created. This statement of work may be very formal or very informal, as long as a work breakdown structure, and the requirements for that work can be derived from it. It is the project manager's job to provide that derivation.

The Work Breakdown Structure (WBS)

As part of defining the work to be done, it is helpful to create a diagram of the total job. This chart, called a work breakdown structure, is a convenient way to display and sum up all the activities and resources needed to do each part of the job, and to break them down into the lowest work package level. A project work breakdown structure looks like an organization chart, but organizes work and resources rather than people. The work breakdown structure with its dictionary (which is akin to the charter that goes with each block on a table of organization) defines all the work required. Every element of work deemed necessary to implement the project must be accounted for. Deliverable products and services generally provide the organizing principle for the WBS, with activities needed to create them as sub-elements under those products.

The work breakdown structure serves four related purposes. The first is to keep track of all elements of the work to be done in the project during both the planning and execution phases. It is a framework for assuring that nothing has been forgotten, and therefore defines the project statement of work.   Second, it provides a structure for costing each element of work for the contract. Time-phased resources are priced and budgeted at every level of the WBS. Third, the same structure should be used during the project implementation to accumulate the actual costs as they are incurred; these will be compared to the time-phased budgeted resources for assessing progress and cost performance.   Fourth, it is a structure for determining what disciplines are required and relating organizational responsibilities to the work to be done.

Partial Work Breakdown Structure

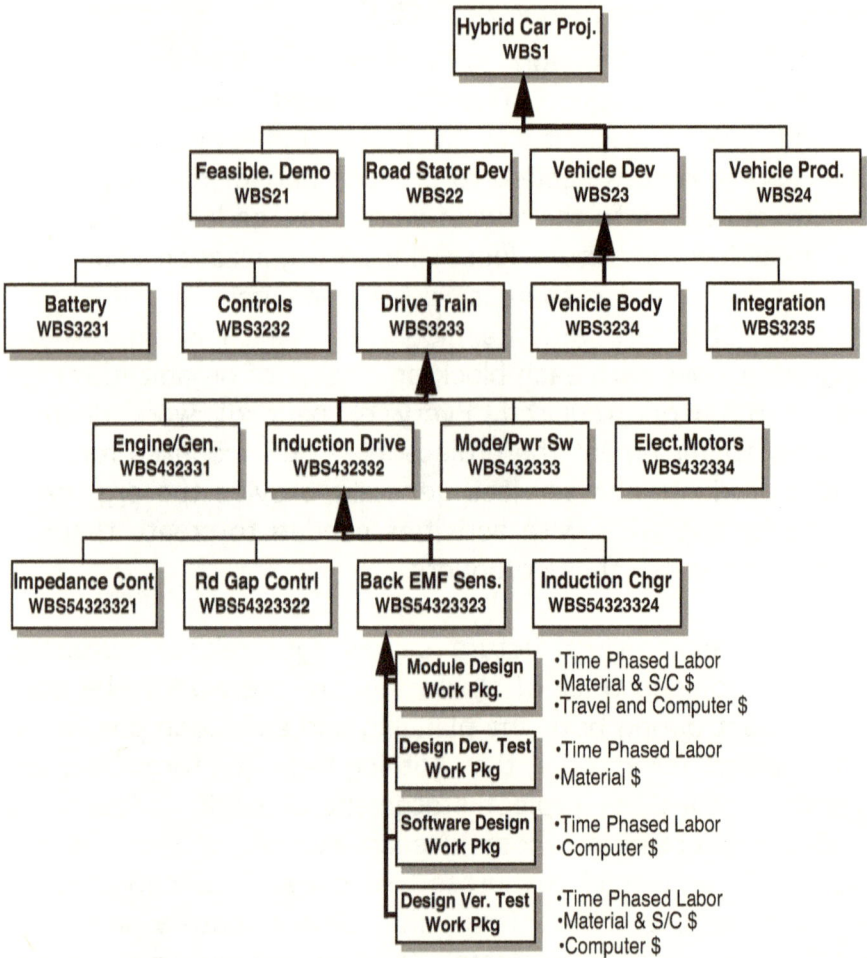

Figure 7-1 A Simplified Work Breakdown Structure Example

Figure 7-1 shows a simplified partial work breakdown structure example for the development of a fictitious new hybrid automobile. Only one twig of one branch of the actual WBS is shown. Note that while not shown, each end-item product element of the WBS occurs twice; once for the non-recurring development tasks, and again under vehicle production for the recurring costs, where only the cost of repetitively producing the vehicle is gathered. The importance of this is that if the product has a target unit production cost, that cost must be allocated and budgeted among all its parts and the cost accumulation system imposed to gather actuals against the estimates under these recurring cost elements. This will be discussed further under design to unit production cost methodology in section 7.4.4.

Developing the Program Anatomy

One of the most important elements of the program planning and implementation process is the creation and maintenance of the master schedule or anatomy of the project or program. In order for the personnel working on each part of the project to do the detailed task planning, scheduling and costing consistently and compatibly with other parts of the project, the over-all anatomy and ground rules must be developed and adjusted as the elements of the project develop their responsive plans.

This section discusses the general steps to get from an overall rough plan to detailed time phased task definition and time phased resource plans. A missile development program is used as an example where many production units are planned and perhaps 32 units must be expended during development to prove the design. While the time scales and quantities may differ for different types of products, the rhythm is similar and generally determined by the time to acquire parts. Given a preliminary set of functional requirements, this schedule provides for a first flight 36 months from go ahead. EMD or engineering manufacturing development is Pentagon-ese for development for production and LRIP stands for Low Rate Initial Production.

.

Development Program Flow

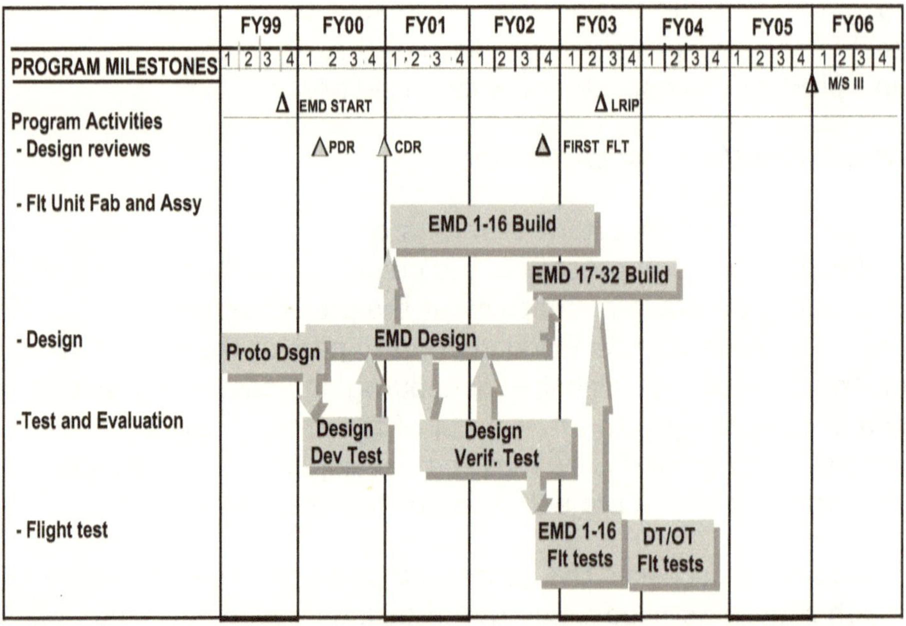

PROGRAM MILESTONES	FY99	FY00	FY01	FY02	FY03	FY04	FY05	FY06
	1 2 3 4	1 2 3 4	1 2 3 4	1 2 3 4	1 2 3 4	1 2 3 4	1 2 3 4	1 2 3 4

Program Activities
- Design reviews

Δ EMD START   Δ LRIP   Δ M/S III

ΔPDR ΔCDR   Δ FIRST FLT

- Flt Unit Fab and Assy

EMD 1-16 Build

EMD 17-32 Build

- Design

Proto Dsgn   EMD Design

-Test and Evaluation

Design Dev Test   Design Verif. Test

- Flight test

EMD 1-16 Flt tests   DT/OT Flt tests

Figure 7-2

The Anatomy of a Typical Development Project

Figure 7-2 illustrates the rhythm of design evolution, test, and revision that is required in a sample missile development project. tests are needed to evaluate the design over the full range of operations. It takes about 6 months to create a design and breadboard it to verify that it performs as anticipated. This is true whether it be electronics, electromechanical equipment, ordnance, or purely mechanical structure.

Testing the interactions of a missile with its environment requires flying and expending it, and many complete flights.

Figure 7-3 shows a missile subsystem development plan that
supports the prior missile development plan of figure 7-2.

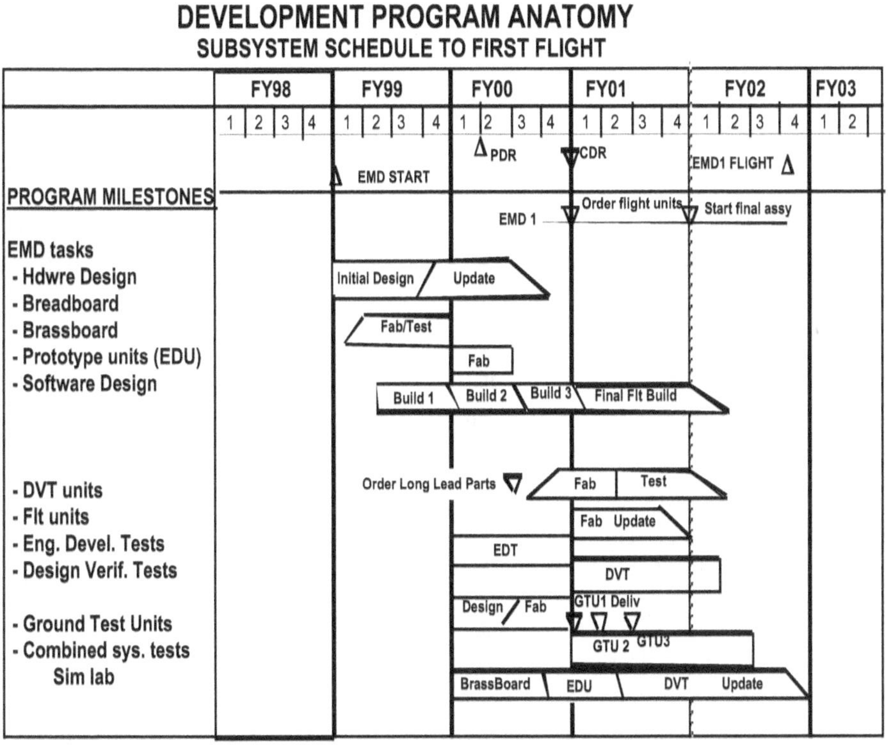

DEVELOPMENT PROGRAM ANATOMY
SUBSYSTEM SCHEDULE TO FIRST FLIGHT

Figure 7-3 Typical Subsystem Plan

When breadboards are complete and brass boards are being
completed and the mechanical packaging has been   designed,
preliminary drawings can be released to build the prototypes
to be used for engineering evaluation test (EDT).   When envi-
ronmental testing has completed, any fixes needed can be

incorporated by Engineering Change Order to the supplier or fabricating organization during the fab of initial flight and design verification (DVT) units.

The Ground Test Units (GTU) are flight configuration vehicles that never fly but are used for various integration tests. In this plan the first GTU will be built up using engineering development units (EDU) which will be built for that purpose. The second GTU will use design verification test (DVT) hardware which is flight quality hardware which will be tested to verify the design is ready for flight. The third GTU may use DVT units initially and can then be upgraded with flight hardware if required. In any case hardware will be designated for all GTUs and the Simulation laboratory on a non-conflict basis.

In general, custom chips produced by foundries will be the pacing item in electronics packages during early development. Mechanical design and printed wiring boards can be designed and ordered during this time with first use being in brass boards to verify proper heat transfer, noise compatibility and acceptable operation. Flight1 software is to be developed with the hardware by the same IPT and is to have all tactical mission functionality in it from build 1 and up. There will be no incomplete software builds for EMD flights. Updates will be made as required during the EMD program but only for findings from flight or to meet new requirements which will be changes in scope. You can now begin to see how the planning process defines the internal contracts between the various members of the project.

With the level of detail in the subsystem plan above, 3T charts (task, talent, time) can be developed to establish the time phased resources for each task needed to accomplish the work defined. This is a negotiated plan and considers the risk involved in doing the job for the resources negotiated as well as the project milestones supported by each task against which accomplishment will be measured. Examples of such spread sheets created on Excel are shown in chapter 8.

Program Integration Media

I personally like to use what I call a **Program Requirements Manual (PRM)** to provide a road map to the entire project. It is a living document. By that I mean that it is a continuously evolving loose-leaf bound document with frequent page changes and additions, and a change notice page that accompanies each change. Every page has a signature block for the Program Manager. Copies are maintained in the office of every activity leader involved in the program. Updates can be sent by e-mail, but the books must be hard copy. If someone new to the activity were to pick up this book at any point in time, it would lead them to any detail of the program. It comes into being at the time the project implementation begins, incorporating and providing the means of updating the program plan.

The PRM has an introduction containing the purpose and objectives of the project. Presumably, these rarely change. It then lists all requirements documents that govern what is being done. These include contractual documents and master specifications, as well as any internal contracts or ground rules that were commitments for the program during its formulation. These are listed in order of precedence -- that is, which governs in case of conflict. As specific decisions are made over time that either flesh out details of implementation or modify existing details, these are coordinated and issued over the program manager's signature as **program management memos.**

These memos, which can be numbered according to the elements of the work breakdown structure, become page additions in the program requirements manual. Anyone working on the program can initiate a program management memo, but it must be coordinated with every potentially affected organization as shown by their authorized signature, and can only be issued when signed by the Project Manager or his or her designee. In all cases, in addition to describing an agreed upon action, there must be a budget statement, which says either " This will be accomplished within existing budget" or "budget for this task will be provided by___". You can see that each memo is a negotiation and contract among the affected parties. If the program manager ever signs and issues a unilateral program management memo, it is like issuing a blank check.

The Program Requirements Manual contains as references, the current versions of key product implementation and design guidance documents, which are issued and controlled by the organizations that create them. Note that the program manager does not control or approve those implementing documents, but includes the reference to latest version as part of the road map into the product design and implementation.

Program Configuration Control - Block Change and Coordination

Periodically, the program plan is updated by block change, usually when some significant change or event occurs. The promulgation of this change is by Program Management Memo with narrative describing the changes to the program and the master schedule baseline designation by a change letter. Typically, budget revisions are made at this time as well, reflecting agreements or decisions based on the progress to date and problems encountered. Changes may be made to reduce cost, or in some cases the program manager may budget more work out of his or her management reserve.

Product Manufacturing Scheduling and Programming

Product Manufacturing Scheduling and programming must be undertaken soon after the project starts. While the details of the design of the various product parts may not yet be known, it is crucial to create the picture of what has to be built, bought, and stocked, and how and when it will be done. Usually the first product articles to be built will be used in design evaluation testing at various levels, and these hardware requirements are an output of the integrated test plan described in section 7.2. Figure 7-4 shows a typical program planning chart taken from an actual program plan. In this production planning example,

PLANNING FOR PRODUCTION

	FY99	FY00	FY01	FY02	FY03	FY04	FY05	FY06
	1 2 3 4	1 2 3 4	1 2 3 4	1 2 3 4	1 2 3 4	1 2 3 4	1 2 3 4	1 2 3 4
PROGRAM **MILESTONES**	△PROJ. START	CRITICAL DESIGN REVIEW ▽		△ 1ST FLT	△LRIP AUTH.		FULL PROD △ AUTH.	FUE △
• DEVELOPMENT	DEV. DESIGN		MFR 16 EMD FLT TEST UNITS	PROD. DESIGN				
• ACQUISITION	PLACE ORDERS ▽	START F/A ▽	▽1ST DELIVERY	40 LRIP UNITS				
				48 LRIP UNITS				

Figure 7-4 Production Planning Example

that purports to show a logical project phasing into low rate initial production.

"Low rate initial production" (LRIP) is a commitment to the first limited number of production missiles prior to completion of evaluation testing. Their purpose is to ramp up manufacturing rate at all suppliers and contractor production facilities to assure that the implementation of those increased rates do not introduce undesired changes in the production article and that affordability targets are in fact being met, before full production is implemented.

A slightly different display method of the same plan on the next chart will show it to be wrong. Figure 7-5 shows an approach I would recommend remembering when you start to lay out programs where significant development leading to a significant production run is to occur.

Figure 7-5 displays the production schedule in a more meaningful way, and we can now see the fallacy of the plan, The parallelograms are a technique I like to use to show the production "waterfall" when you plan to build a significant number of units. If each unit build were a horizontal line broken into the two phases shown, the loci of placing orders, start of fab and assembly, and delivery would form the parallelograms shown. The vertical scale is 10 product units per division, and the horizontal scale is time where in this case divisions are quarters of a year. While in reality, products are typically bought and built in lots, the parallelogram shows the "just in time" dates for each unit. The milestone FUE at the upper right stands for "First Unit Equipped" and refers to the full complement of systems available to the first operational combat battalion for this missile program example.

The first thing we see that there is an 18 month gap in operations between the start of the last development unit and the start of the first Low rate initial production units both at suppliers and in fab and assembly. What are all those manufacturing people at suppliers and in our own facility going to do during the 18 month stand down? They are going to other jobs, and may never be back. The result? You don't buy what you tested, because manufacturing continuity has been lost. Moreover, quadrupling the production rate after that gap is likely to be problematic.

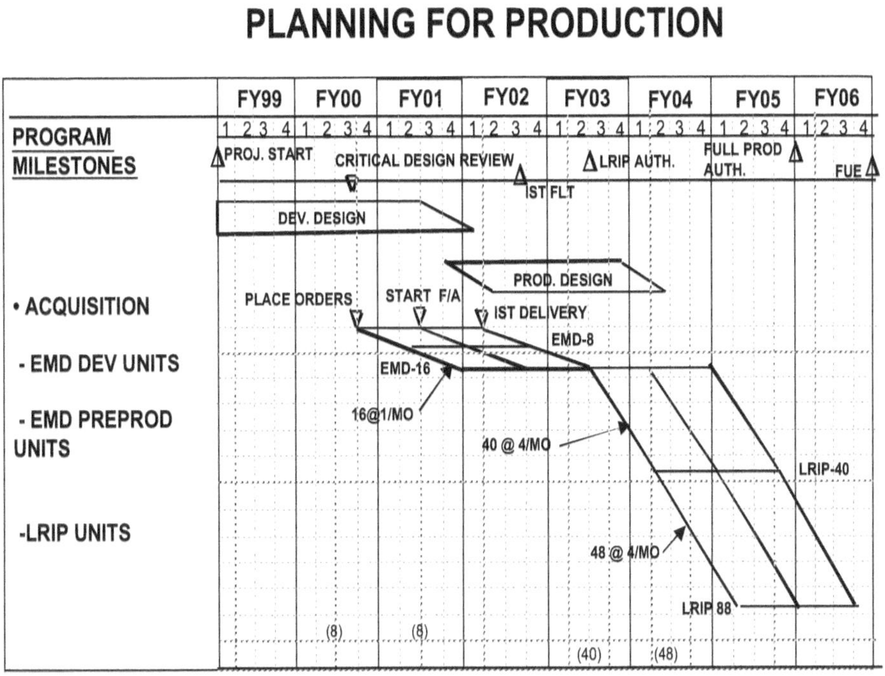

PLANNING FOR PRODUCTION

	FY99	FY00	FY01	FY02	FY03	FY04	FY05	FY06

Figure 7-5 A More Useful Display

A Better Plan

Figure 7-6 is a much more rational production plan that meets the same goals with continuity of manufacture from development into production. We have added pre-production missiles built during EMD to demonstrate that when missiles are built to the intended product disclosure, those missiles can be built and will perform as anticipated.

PLANNING FOR PRODUCTION

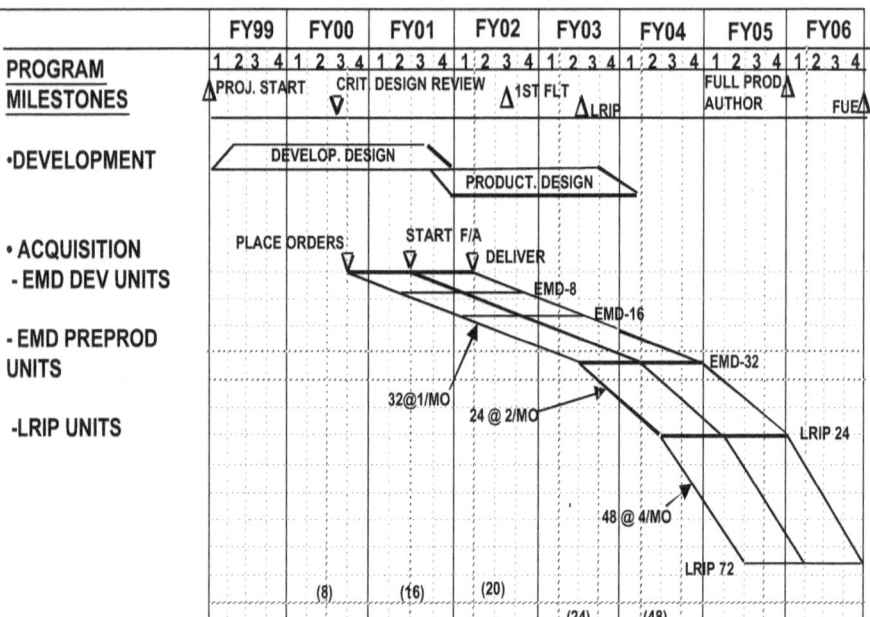

Figure 7-6   A better Plan

Proofing of production tools, processes, and facilities as well as the paper are accomplished with these vehicles.

Problems are addressed and corrected before low rate initial production missiles are procured. Some of these vehicles can fulfill the requirements for customer operational evaluation as well.

By displaying the plan in this way, you can quickly see where problems lie and how to plan major design milestones consistent with a plan that provides continuity of operations.

Production lots can be planned as well as when funding must be available for each lot.

In order to establish the lead times and spans depicted in the parallelograms of figure 7-6 evaluation of the purchasing, fabrication, and assembly sequence for each part of the product must be undertaken. This process, typically called programming the job, generates a whole "tree" of lower-level documentation for every segment of the product. This data set includes the operations planning, manufacturing methods and processes; tooling to be used; determination of need dates for start of next assembly; fabrication spans and start dates; purchasing lead times, order dates for buying and kitting of the bill of materials; and job instructions.

All subassemblies and assemblies of the end product are identified by drawing number, and a manufacturing / assembly sequence and job programming chart is created. This is another form of work breakdown structure. In one respect this chart is a subset of the recurring part of the overall project WBS. It identifies what work has to be done at each level of product manufacture and assembly along with the applicable configuration management information. Eventually, for every part number, it becomes the top document of a set that captures the detailed job definitions and shop paper for every manufacturing operation, assembly operation and job instruction.

A partial and very simplified example for a hybrid automobile might look like Figure 7-7. The actual chart is, of course, much larger. For each segment or subassembly, the various functional organizations that add value to that segment commit to a plan for their part of the activity, using this work breakdown as the framework for job package planning and authorization.

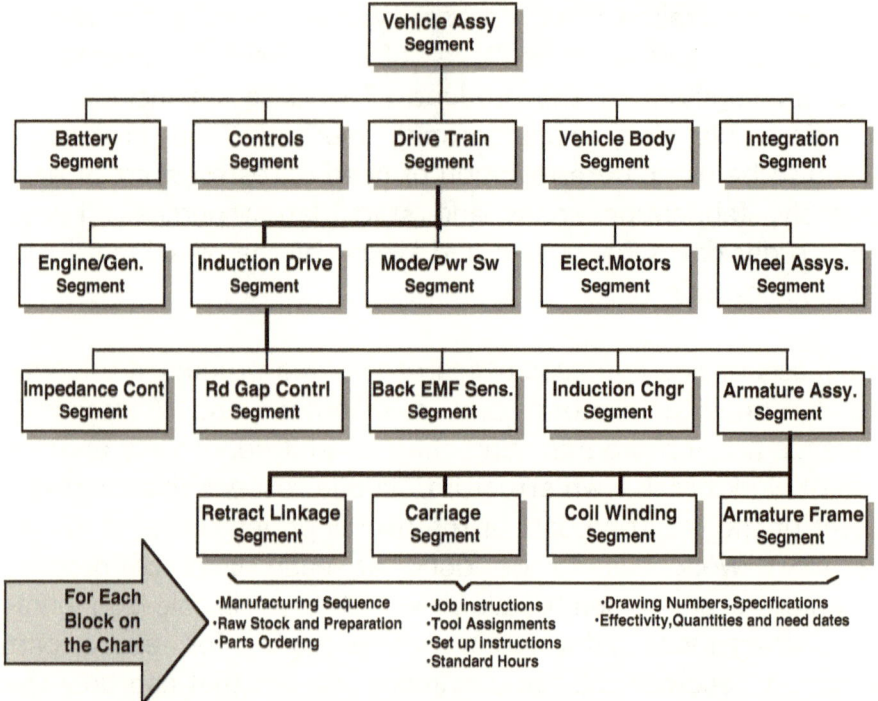

Partial Vehicle Job Assignment Manufacturing/Assembly Chart

Figure 7-7   A simplified Manufacturing/Assembly Sequence Chart

For the manufacturing planning and scheduling process required to prepare to build a run of product, the Operations organizations (Manufacturing, Procurement and Quality Assurance) need detailed design disclosure data, which, while not yet released, must be pretty mature. They are going to generate an entire production documentation set, job instructions, tooling, and order plans based on that data and the commitment of when final design data will be available for that particular segment.

Consequently, they don't want to even start the product master scheduling activity until the engineering data is mature. At the same time, new tools and facilities may be required and these often have long lead times

Engineering, on the other hand, will not want to commit until it can confidently predict that the design is mature. On the third hand, we have the project manager and the customer service folks, who have to make commitments about when the product deliveries will occur, and in many cases plan and reserve outside services and facilities. They cannot afford to find out that the plan cannot be achieved after the fact. This conflict in equally valid objectives is fundamental and one of the most difficult to manage.

Since nothing can proceed without the design data, the responsible engineering organization must commit to a time when preliminary design data will be available, when "OK to buy to" lists of materials will be available. They must also commit when the design will be released for manufacture, based on completion of development prototype testing and correction of any problems found during those tests. Agreements must be made on what kind of change control will be used during the transition from building experimental product hardware until design release.

On the basis of this preliminary planning data, Purchasing must estimate order placement dates, and delivery spans for all components, raw materials, and outside supplied sub assemblies. Manufacturing and Quality Assurance must begin creating skeleton work instructions and manufacturing planning for the creation of each and every segment including design of tooling. Estimates are created for the manufacturing spans needed assuming all raw materials and purchased parts are on hand when needed. On the basis of the resulting data, shop loading and tooling requirements can be determined and hiring of any required additional talent planned.

When I ran large programs, I would insist that Engineering and Operations had to begin this manufacturing programming process within six months of starting the project, and complete it by the end of the first year. They, of course, thought I was insane.   But it was imperative to validate the project master schedule assumptions about lead times, order dates, etc. which, until validated, were based purely on prior program experience. That should be sufficient, but as we have said several times, until you have buy-in and commitment from those who are going to do the job, you have nothing real. And there is an axiom that seems to apply to every project: No matter who signed up to what in the proposal and initial plan, there will be a host of individuals and groups who will tell you that it can't possibly be done once you have committed to do it. So, I wasn't insane -- just not willing to fly blind..

Once we got by the point of talking past each other over this dilemma, we arrived at an uneasy but workable solution -- to add a *preliminary* product manufacturing scheduling phase, ahead of the formal programming. While this entailed added work, it created a preliminary skeleton plan, which, together with "producibility teams," (forerunners of what are now called integrated product teams) working together from the onset, provided the continuing visibility to the Operations organizations as the design evolved. This in turn allowed Operations to do much of the detailed planning, influence the design, and identify design constraints. Thus they were able to proceed on key tasks such as tooling design and more importantly to make commitments on manufacturing time spans. This whole concept of concurrency and integrated product development teams is sometimes referred to as concurrent engineering.

A formal chairman or czar is needed to keep this process on track and to keep all the necessary feet to the fire. This must be a respected person who has the knowledge and authority to incentivize people to find solutions when they reach an impasse. The end result of this preliminary product manufacturing scheduling effort is a negotiated baseline schedule for the creation of both the design data and the product; this activity will either validate the overall project master schedule or modify it. The result is a set of commitments that every activity literally signs up to, based on the commitments made by all the others. Experience has shown this approach to yield about 90% fidelity to what actually results. Moreover, if things change from these preliminary programming assumptions, the implications of those changes are better understood.

Internal Contracts -- Change Control

The key principle in all that we have discussed so far is the establishment and maintenance of an integrated, running contract with all participating parties. This is a contract that reflects program decisions made, and advises everyone involved that those decisions have been made. Again, note that we are not talking about design decisions, but about program implementation decisions. The same thing is true of manufacturing processes to be used. In each case, the result is a set of commitments against which accomplishment will be measured by the responsible management. The product manufacturing scheduling process generates contracts among the activities that depend on each other. Unilateral legislation of these plans by program or senior management does not result in commitments or ownership. The process described here does.

Design and Configuration Change Control

One of the important features of the internal contract set is a rigorous system for managing changes in the product configuration. This discipline is often referred to as configuration management. It is a formal process for evaluating proposed changes for their impact on the project as a whole, including the necessity, what the cost and schedule implications are, and when they will be introduced into the process.

The change control process thus ensures coordination with all potentially affected parties before the change is approved, indicates the changes in the internal contracts that will be required, and finally provides for the paper and hardware trail for the introduction of that change. The reason for including it under project integration rather than product integration is the fact that design changes usually have far reaching project implications that may not be evident to the originator.

7.2 Program Evaluation (Program status, and control)

Whether a project's or program's end-products, are hardware, software, or services, there are three basic measures of accomplishment: *technical performance, cost performance* and *schedule performance.* *Technical performance* is the accomplishment of the requirements of the task, as outlined in the statement of work. *Cost performance* is the cost of accomplishment of the work when compared to the bid or budgeted cost. If production unit price is an important attribute (and it usually is), cost performance would include real measures of that cost prior to and early in actual production. *Schedule performance* is when the work is accomplished compared to the master schedule.

Program evaluation is the process of determining whether the requirements of the project are being met, and if they are being accomplished on schedule and at the budgeted cost. And when targets are not being met, it is program evaluation's job to recommend corrective actions.

Technical Performance Assessment

As the project progresses, the program manager and his or her management team must have visibility into how well the evolving product will meet the requirements of the project. This requires some form of ongoing assessment. It is often called technical performance measurement, and is best accomplished by creating a formal process for periodic review of every part of the end product during its development. The chief project engineer, who is responsible for the product design, should be the source of this evaluation, using the framework of a requirements breakdown structure. This third form of product WBS, rather than defining the work and resources necessary to create the product, defines the product's function or use. It is used to allocate requirements as discussed in section 7.3. A proven technique for technical performance assessment is discussed in section 7.4.

Cost and Schedule Status and Control

Part of the process of initiating project work is the authorizing of budgets into the accounting system of the Enterprise for all organizations involved in the project. These budgets will be structured in cost accounts keyed to the work breakdown structure and the organizations implementing those elements of work. During the planning phase of the project, these budgets should have been planned on a time-phased basis by resource type for the entire project duration. If done properly, on day one of the project these resource plans are activated in the accounting system and are the budget baseline that goes with the current baseline program plan. All the schedule milestones are based on the program master schedule and will be used as the yardstick for measuring accomplishment.

Accomplishment Measures -- Earned Value Systems and Milestones,

It is important to use cost and schedule plans and actual costs and accomplishment to assess progress on the project. One of the most effective means of measuring progress in a large project is the use of an earned value system. This type of system, has been required in some form on most Department of Defense cost-reimbursable contracts.

The system uses the budgeted cost to accomplish each component of work by the scheduled time as the measure of planned accomplishment. The planned or budgeted cost of the actual work performed and the actual cost of work performed compared to the budgeted cost of scheduled work are measures of cost and schedule variance from plan that signal potential problems. A description of a typical earned value measurement system is discussed in chapter 8.

Sometimes maligned as an unnecessary burden, an earned value system as the primary cost management system is a very powerful tool in measuring accomplishment and foreseeing cost and schedule problems before they become evident by other means. I found it helpful to use this type of system even on company-funded projects, without the excessive government-mandated variance report preparation that most users find burdensome. The disadvantage of earned-value systems is that this capability must be integrated with the Enterprise accounting system in order for the data to be reliable and effectively used.

Product Definition Disciplines

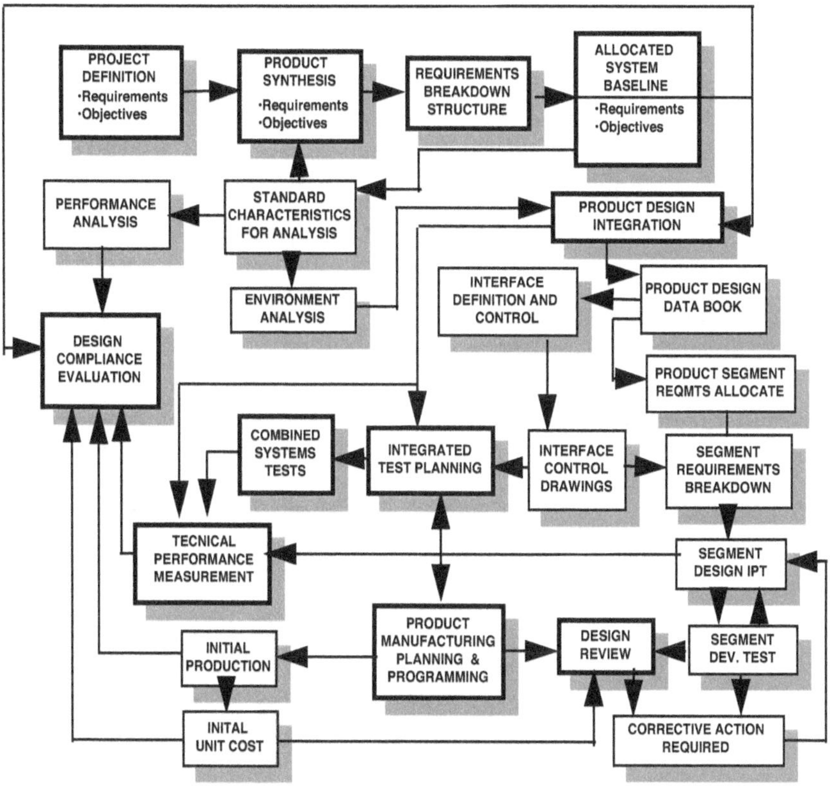

Figure 7-8 Product Definition Disciplines

7.3 Product Definition

Figure 7-8 illustrates the disciplines and their relationships needed to create an integrated product definition.

Systems Engineering Requirements Definition, & Allocation

Earlier in the book, we noted that engineering tends to be organized along the lines of the product elements. Systems engineering is therefore a crucial overarching discipline in any complex project where several product elements are involved. As a result, regardless of where the systems engineers report in the organizational structure, they must recognize that they are, among other things, the program manager's technical staff. Design authority is delegated to the appropriate product segment design teams along with the responsibility for meeting their allocated requirements. This section presents some of the important functions that the project manager depends on the systems engineers to perform.

A. Standard Characteristics for analysis and performance assessment

In products that involve complex systems and interactions, it is important to use the same system description for all the analytical work that is being done to either set requirements or evaluate how the product design will perform. One way to do this is to have a configuration for analysis that is controlled and only changed as a block so that everyone stays on the same page so to speak.

A tool that we used for this purpose was called the Standard Characteristics for Analysis. This document is controlled by the systems engineering organization with inputs from each subsystemand is revised periodically when substantial physical configuration and/or functional changes have accumulated in the product that could affect simulations, software or previous analysis.

B. Functional analysis and requirements definition and allocation

One of the first things that must be done as a project begins the design synthesis process is to allocate all the required attributes of the product among all of its component parts. A tool for assisting in allocating requirements and later evaluating the design compliance with them is the requirements breakdown structure that defines the allocated baseline. Let's take our hybrid automobile as an example.

Hybrid Vehicle Partial Requirements Tree or Breakdown Structure Example

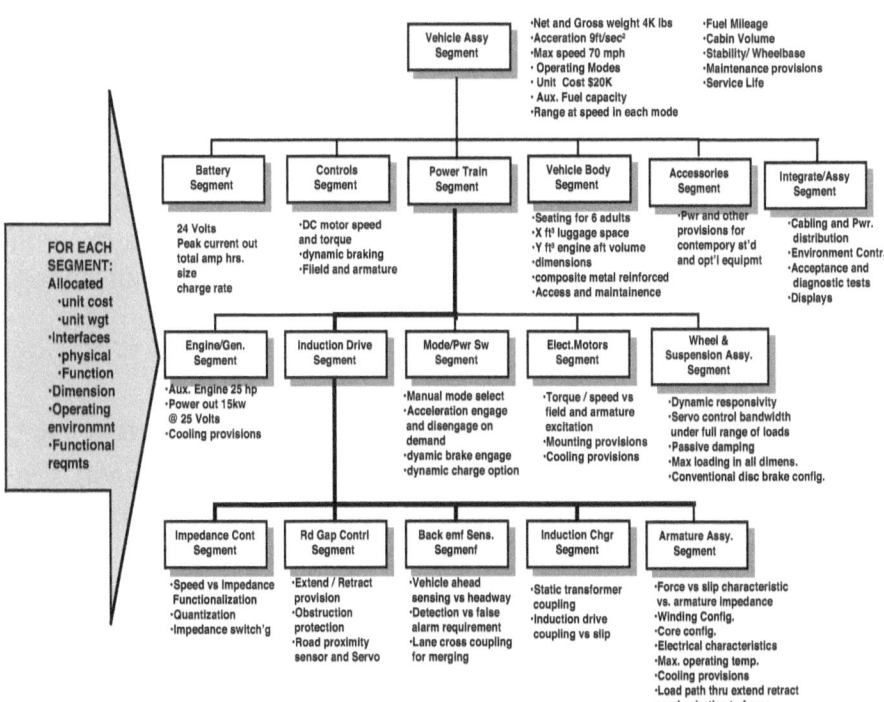

Figure 7-9 A Sample Requirements Breakdown Structure

Figure 7-9 shows a partial and simplified requirements break-down for this vehicle. As with other examples in this chapter, I have only expanded part of the tree; if complete it would take several pages. Also what is shown is largely qualitative, as it might be early in design synthesis, rather than quantitative as it would need to be at completion.

Some of the attributes are: battery size and capacity, accelera-tion, fuel mileage, service life, maintenance requirements, weight allocations, and especially unit cost. Dimensions, stability, cabin volume and seating capacity are also important.

Design Integration

One of the most important design disciplines is the design inte-gration function. Given a set of design requirements and a design concept, those requirements must be parceled out among the elements of the design, and the interfaces between the elements defined, controlled and validated. Also included in this discipline is the definition and control of product external interfaces for handling, receiving power, operating, monitoring, and testing if required.

A. Design Integration and Data

Several tools can help to perform this integration. One, is a product design data book, with a section devoted to each seg-ment of the product as a design guide. This is distributed to each subsystem or segment design team. It is used to document and disseminate the allocations of attributes and derived re-quirements, such as physical and functional interfaces, and induced environments that must be met by each segment based on the evolving design. Typically, this Data Book is, like the Pro-gram Requirements Manual, a living document that can be updated and augmented with additional pages as the design progresses. All applicable design requirements are included or referenced in this data book. Key subsystem requirements documents are referenced but not controlled in the Data Book as they are developed, in the same way that the Data Book is referenced but not controlled in the Program Requirements Manual.

B. Key Attributes allocation (Functions, Unit Cost, Product life and Reliability, Tolerances etc.)

This allocation process is initiated with targets using comparable experience from past work, while holding a reserve to relieve problems where the cost to achieve a target is too high. Then it must be an iterative process with the design teams to evaluate the difficulty and cost of meeting them in each area. Tolerance allocation should normally be statistically combined rather than added worst on worst, to avoid unreasonable cost.

C. Interface definitions internal and external

Interface definitions between segments of the product and external to the product are documented with Interface Control Documents. These include tolerances on critical dimensions established by tolerance analysis, characteristics and tolerances of functional interface signals and power etc.

D, Configuration Change Control

An important systems engineering role in its dual capacity as design integrator and project technical staff is to chair the change control process described earlier in section 7.1.6. This process while not explicitly shown in figure 7-8 can be thought of as an overlay to that schematic that assures that proposed design changes whatever their source, are evaluated for their effect on every part of the process shown in that schematic.

E. Participation in test planning

While many test requirements are generated by each product segment, it is important that systems engineering integrate those test requirements to assure test completeness and that assembly-level tests are perceptive in verifying the function of the product system for its intended use. This can be done by creating a total product test requirements specification that is the top spec for all test requirements and invokes all segment test specs for both development and in process production tests.

One can see from the foregoing discussion, that the overarching disciplines generally grouped under systems engineering span across all other activities, keeping them coordinated as the product design evolves, and providing configuration control discipline for the integrated design. Systems Engineering looks at the interactions between product segments and between the product and the environment in which it will be used. The individual product teams must recognize the importance of this function and rely on the systems engineering member of their team to tie back to other teams.

The use of integrated product teams creates the connection between the design task expertise and the producing and user expertise from the beginning of the design activity. As a result, when a problem is encountered, no matter where in the anticipated life cycle or segment of the product, the integrating disciplines, properly used, will register it and cause a decision to be made about its disposition. The next section shows how that part of the process works.

7.4 Product Evaluation

Design Performance Evaluation

A. Technical performance measurement - Use of the requirements work breakdown structure

We will evaluate technical performance against the allocated baseline. As previously mentioned, one way of organizing and tracking these allocated requirements is through the use of a requirements breakdown structure.

**Technical Performance Measurement
System Schematic**

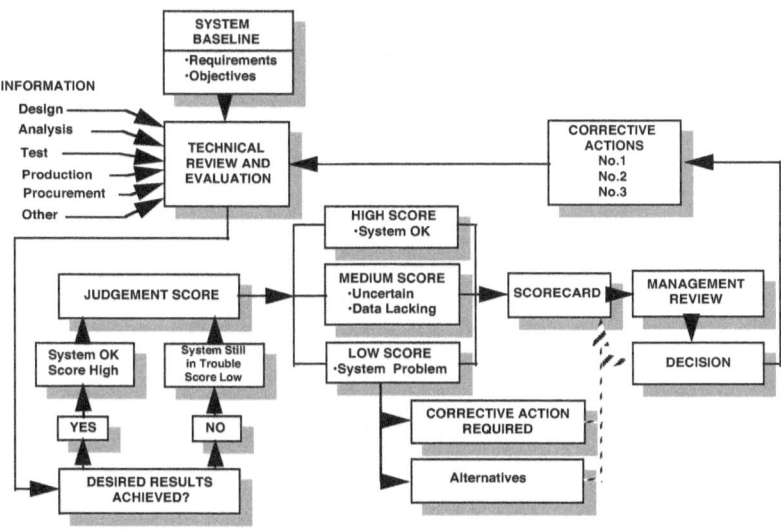

Figure 7-10 A Technical Performance Measurement System

The scoring system we have employed uses a rating system of 1 to 5. with the following definitions: Sometimes red, orange, yellow green and blue are used.

An effective method for implementing technical performance is depicted in figure 7.10. This system is maintained in the project systems engineering organization by personnel knowledgeable about the attributes that have been allocated, the design process, and system interactions. In an integrated product team environment, these could be the systems engineering members on each product segment team. The technique requires self-reporting and allows a continuous objective evaluation of the status of the product design in achieving the project requirements defined in the allocated baseline requirements breakdown structure.

1 or red - Major problem requiring management attention and help needed. Current design will not meet requirement. No corrective action identified

2 or orange - Significant problem with no immediate management action needed; no plan for corrective action but evaluation continuing. Watch this space.

3 or yellow - Potential problem in meeting requirement, limited data available, corrective action plan exists, results will determine rating.

4 or green - Current design appears satisfactory based on results thus far Minor problems if any have been worked out, solutions exist and are in progress. Evaluation tests not complete. No corrective action needed.

5 or blue - Current design is in good shape. Design evaluation tests completed and no problems remain.

Additionally, a circle around the rating signifies that a corrective action plan exists but has not yet been implemented or completed. A subscript number is displayed with the three lower ratings to remind viewers of the number of weeks the rating has existed.

This assessment when taken together with cost and schedule status gives an overall picture of the program health at any time. All attributes, including unit production cost, are included in this evaluation process.

The presentation of status using this approach is done on an exception basis. Problem areas are tracked using an indentured presentation chart approach. While gathered and evaluated by the systems engineering personnel, the system is fed by the ongoing design, analysis, and test activities. This information can be presented to the chief project engineer and all responsible engineering managers at a weekly project engineering status meeting with every product segment or element covered at least once per month. While it is a self-evaluation system, its integrity is assured by the fact that the engineering management and program management, who should be aware of most events on the program are in a position to evaluate the evaluation itself, as it is given. If the designers have not 'fessed up to a problem to the evaluator, or if the evaluator has not done an adequate assessment, it soon becomes obvious.

B Product Requirements Compliance

As the technical staff of the project manager, the systems engineering requirements group has a responsibility for devising an evaluation plan for assuring that the product as designed will comply with the requirements. This may require a combination of testing, analysis, and simulation. As part of this charge, the

systems engineers who will do this evaluation should get together with the independent test and evaluation group to create a
plan taking full advantage of the test team's expertise as well as
their own.

Integrated test program planning

For any project, whether a large building, a large software program, or the development of a hybrid car, perceptive testing is
an important part of the design evaluation. It is important to
establish criteria for properly testing the various elements of the
product so confidence in each of the parts that make up the
whole is equally high.

To assure that the proper tests are planned to evaluate the
product design and to assure planning for sufficient hardware
and software and test equipment for all testing including the element development tests, it is very desirable to have an
"Integrated Test Program Plan". Regardless of who has the responsibility or need for a test, it must be accounted for in this
plan. In addition, after development has been completed, and
the product design is released for production, the in-process
tests must be provided for as well.

In our model, we charge the Test and Evaluation organization,
the independent test agency during development, with the creation and maintenance of the integrated test plan. This includes
the common development test strategy to be used. The quality
assurance organization will be the independent testing agency
during production.

A. Development test consistency

A common set of defined test objectives tailored to the unique
nature of each component or process provides guidance to the
design and test teams so that oversights are minimized. The

following division of responsibilities has been found to work well for complex projects.

B. Subsystem or Segment Development Test Requirements

The cognizant product subsystem or element engineering group is responsible for defining the development tests needed to create their element of the product with confidence. This includes informal experimental tests and prototyping. They also define what tests are needed for design verification: that is, those tests run on the first article built to the released design disclosure. However, commencing with design verification testing, the test organization is responsible for conduct of the test to the engineering requirements.

C. Integration or Combined System Testing

For combined systems-level testing, systems engineering defines the test requirements in a "Test Requirements Specification" and the Test Organization is responsible for designing and conducting these tests.

D. In process test consistency

The same philosophy applies to in process testing. When the product is ready to produce, QA has the responsibility for in process testing at all levels, building on the methods used during the development phase of the project.

E. Test Hardware Requirements

The Test and Evaluation organization should create and maintain an up to date test hardware requirements list as part of the Integrated Test Program Plan. This list establishes all the various units of subsystem and total system hardware needed to complete the integrated test program. This plan, of course, requires input from all groups working on the project, and allows multiple usage of hardware and test equipment where feasible to save the cost of duplicating hardware.

On the other hand, one of the most common mistakes in projects is not recognizing that failures occur during development, and not providing enough hardware to support the necessary test and evaluation activities. Penny-wise and pound-foolish. The list should provide for appropriate spares to assure that losses during test do not hamper the overall program with hardware shortages.

Product Liability Evaluation

In today's litigious environment, product liability has become a major area of concern. Product safety must be a design consideration, and an independent assessment of the resulting design is an important discipline. It is only a slight exaggeration to say that the product will only occasionally be used in the manner intended by the developer. Properly prepared user's manuals (with appropriate warnings on misuse) help, but the product liability evaluation should take to heart the consequences of blatant misuse and mishandling.

Product Unit Cost Evaluation

If you want to achieve a production unit cost target for your product, it must be designed to achieve that cost. To do this requires three things:

First, you must have a means for all of the activities that add cost to the creation of the product to be actively involved in the design process from the onset. Each of three activities must make commitments to targets for their cost contribution. Produceability teams, or Integrated Product Teams as described in Chapter 5 are that mechanism.

Second, you must have a mechanism for allocating cost targets, creating cost estimates, evaluating those estimates by the IPTs, and finally accumulating actual costs against those targets when building samples of the product.

Third, you must have representative samples of the product built early enough to see problems and fix them in the product design disclosure and to prove them out before production begins in earnest.

Design to Unit Cost Process

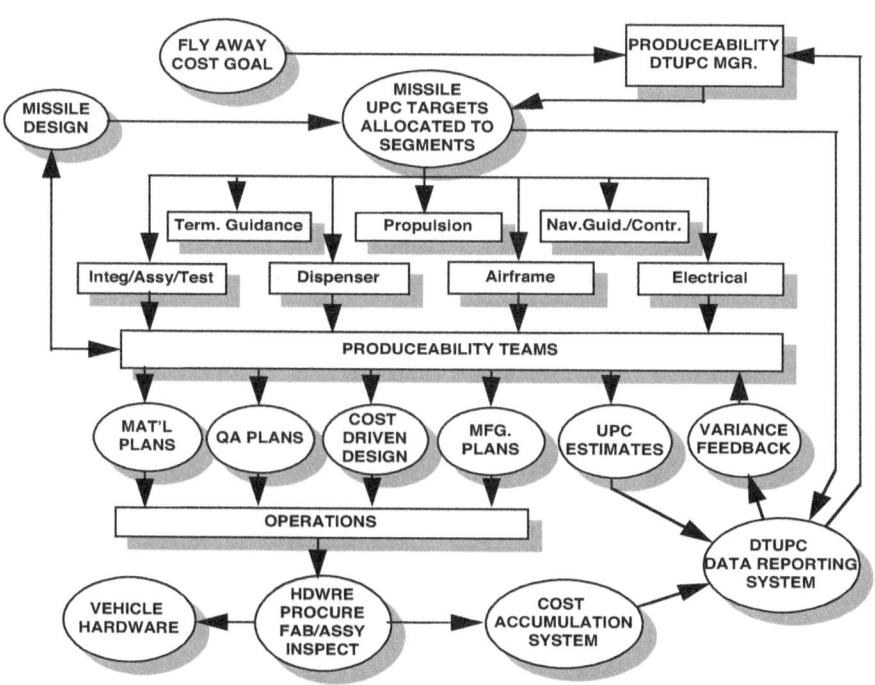

Figure 7-11 Effective Design to Unit Production Cost

Figure 7-11 shows an effective process for designing to unit cost and evaluating progress in achieving those targets. This particular example is from a low cost precision guided missile program.

It is easy to make promises for something that will not be measured for several years. Many design-to-cost programs do just that. As a result, they are not credible and do not achieve their goals. There must be meaningful measurements along the way that validate those promises or they will never be met. An example of the process we instituted on one major defense program is included as Appendix 1. It is the program management memo that implemented the methodology to achieve unit production costs, and it was successful, because it had all the elements mentioned above.

7.5. Other Development Disciplines

Design Notebooks

Design notebooks should be required for all work done on any project. These provide a record of the reasoning behind the designer's decisions and are available for others to see in the event that person gets disabled or departs the project for one reason or another.

Discipline for Design Review Against All Requirements

Design review is a very important check and balance to help assure that there are no oversights in the design process. It is not a dog and pony show, but rather a time when the design should be subjected to tough scrutiny. In this chapter we have talked about requirements that are imposed on the various parts of the project by the integration functions. If *all* the requirements applicable to each segment or subsystem of the product, that are evaluated in the technical performance measurement system were collected, these would constitute the allocated requirements on each segment. This is the checklist that should be used for formal design reviews. Design reviews should be performed for every segment of the product at least twice during its development.

The first review addresses the design concept that has been selected, and examines the requirements check-list against the planned approach, and any feasibility tests, similar product applications, and analysis that support the planned approach. The second review takes place after the completion of development tests and shortly before the design package is to be released to manufacturing and procurement. Here the test results are reviewed and the issue is design confidence. Participants in these reviews include members of the design team, senior representatives from their functional organizations, and representatives of all the overarching disciplines mentioned previously in this chapter. Minutes of the proceedings should be kept and action items recorded for disposition.

Design Configuration Control, Release, and Change Control

Today, most design data resides in a CAD/CAM computer database rather than on drawing paper at the time of its release for procurement or manufacture. While the principles that apply to the discipline required for this data are the same whether on a drawing or a computer screen, it is important that the mechanisms unique to each medium be in place.

As a rule, the design of a product element is fluid and changing rapidly until the completion of prototype hardware testing. Once that point is reached, the design organization is ready to freeze the design. It will therefore be released from the unilateral control of the design function and come under project change control. At that point, the data goes through a rigorous check process by the configuration management function to look for any errors, and assure that parts lists and materiel lists are properly included; it is then "programmed" into the procurement and manufacturing process. The change status is maintained in this central database from then on. The design data package is now programmed for manufacture, and work is authorized with budget and manufacturing instructions.

In the meantime, the same (but unreleased) design data can be used by engineering to authorize the build of design verification test samples identified in the integrated test program plan. It is desirable, but not always possible, to release the design package before these samples are built. In any case, they should be built in the same manner that later articles will be. If nothing else, it is desirable to accept this hardware to the released design data package.

Any changes that are identified as a result of design verification must be programmed through the configuration control function as a formal change, since other hardware has been programmed (if not already built) to the released documentation package. If the change affects form, fit, or function, (interchangeability) then the design must be re-identified to prevent the old design from showing up in the market distribution system. You can see that the subject of configuration control is complex, requiring careful and detailed coordination and management. However, failure to do it well is far less pleasant in the long run.

7.6. Production Disciplines

Product Definition for Planning Purposes

Design release is the formal publication of the design data for manufacture. After this point, any changes must be formally evaluated for impact and effectivity because work is in progress.

Production First Article Master Scheduling

In Section 7.1 we discussed this process in the context of development when the design was still evolving. At this juncture, when we are ready to start production, the product design disclosure is mature and released. It is presumed that the configuration is stable and the only changes that will be introduced are those arising out of manufacturing or processing problems encountered during the "Product Disclosure Demonstration", sometimes called "Proofing".

The end result of this product manufacturing scheduling effort is a negotiated baseline schedule for the creation of product that meets the overall project master schedule or modifies it. Problems usually arise and must be worked out during this process. In large projects, this process can take months and is done segment by segment.

Concurrent engineering with the use of Integrated product teams makes this process easier, because the activity representatives have already been involved in every segment of the design. But, IPT's are not a substitute for formal programming -- a mistake many people make.

Product Disclosure Demonstration

During the product development phase of a project, the product samples that are built are usually manufactured in a low-volume flexible manufacturing environment. Often, the workers in those facilities are more experienced artisans who can relate problems encountered with the design data in the shop, along with solutions they worked out. This is in fact part of the validation process.

When the product design has been tested and validated, and the processes and tooling for volume production and quality assurance are in place, it is wise to "proof" the production process. Proofing seeks to demonstrate that the rate production processes, tools, and environment yield the same product that was tested to validate the design disclosure data during development. The validated design disclosure, together with the rate production process, form what I call the product disclosure-- that is, all the data required to set up and create products that will meet all the product requirements on a continuing basis.

Proofing is the process by which we can validate the entire product disclosure, before actually building up to full rate. The samples of product are called pilot production, or low-rate initial production in the current jargon of the Department of Defense. Regardless of what it is called, the intent is to make sure that the process works as anticipated, and that what comes out of the process is what was desired. Until this proofing has been completed, we cannot be sure that development is complete. In Chapter 12, on contracting, we discuss incentive contracts that use this pilot production as the measurement sample for performance against objectives.

7.7. Checks and Balances by Responsibility Hand-off

In applying the overarching disciplines discussed in this chapter, it is useful to think about the way the gestalt works in successful projects. In Chapter 3, we talked about checks and balances that organizational hand-offs can provide. Now, with the picture of overarching disciplines fresh in our minds we can tie the two ideas together. A key theme in this book is building trust, but not blind trust. Checks and balances are an important part of integral management.

Project Systems Engineering Hand-off to Design Engineering

In Section 7.3, we saw that Systems Engineering provides two kinds of integration. One is the definition and allocation of the performance requirements baseline and evaluation of the product design that results from design engineering against that baseline discussed in 7.3. As such, these people are the technical expertise of the project manager. For that reason, I lean toward having this function answer directly to the project manager, or at least be independent of design engineering management.

The second part of the systems engineering responsibility we called the design integration function (section 7.3.2). This function ties all parts of the design together and looks for under-laps in responsibilities and ways to close those gaps. This should be part of the design engineering function but separate from any subsystem management.

Design Hand-off to Testers

At some point in the development process, as described in Section 7.4.2, the designers should reach a point where they are reasonably happy with what they have done and are ready for design verification. It is desirable at this point to step back and let the separate test and evaluation experts put product built to that design through its paces against the requirements. Design engineering should play a supporting role in this activity, but the Test and Evaluation folks would be responsible for reporting the results against a formal test plan. This design verification is really akin to a preliminary qualification test, but does not really address the production part of the process until later.

Development Engineering Hand-off to Manufacturing

Many businesses use a prototype shop that is part of engineering to build the development specimens to be tested. This could include not only the breadboards, brass boards, and prototypes needed to hone the design, but also the design verification samples. It is my experience that this is a fine approach for everything through the prototypes. But the design verification units should be built, if possible, by the people who will produce the end products, even though it may be in a different production environment.

There are two reasons for this. One is that it keeps the operations people involved in the design process as part of concurrent engineering. The second reason is that it helps guard against the release of a sloppy design data package. If an incomplete or poorly defined design package goes into the programming process discussed in Section 7.1, we are going to soon hear some noise in the system about it. That tends to keep folks on their toes.

Manufacturing Hand-off to Product Assurance

It has long been thought that a separate inspection function guards against manufacturing errors or poor quality ending up in finished products. In recent years, this paradigm has been challenged by the concept that, with appropriate training, the manufacturing operator is capable and motivated to prevent and or correct any mistakes or deviations from an acceptable product. In this model, the quality assurance function is primarily one of auditing to make sure that the process is working.

I have watched this done both ways, and am frankly undecided on this subject. I have no doubt that the new paradigm thesis is correct, and that manufacturing personnel can be motivated to assure quality. My current feeling is that in the early stages of a project manufacturing phase, the more traditional hand-off is desirable because personnel are learning the processes as production rate ramps up. This is true of QA as well. The self-inspection model seems to work best when things have settled into a stable and mature mode, but I have seen problems on projects during their production start-up phase.

Chapter 8 Managing Cost

8.0 Understanding the cost of doing business

Everyone has to be somewhere. So Does Cost.
Effective cost management is everybody's business in a successful Enterprise. The principles of integral management call for contracts between peer managers whose activities are interdependent, between managers and subordinates to whom they have delegated responsibilities, and to whom they have committed the resources and support necessary to discharge those responsibilities.

Many CFO's fail to grasp this concept, and therefore consider financial accounting to be a policing and control organization that assures budget compliance. This is a fallacy of major import. To be sure, the financial accounting organization has an important fiduciary responsibility to the governance of the Enterprise. But finance's proper role recognizes that their organization does not and cannot control anything. For that matter, neither does general management. What they collectively can and must do is incentivize task managers to do what is needed, *and* to provide the tools, data, and visibility to the doing levels of management to enable *them* to manage cost.

Finance can and should integrate and analyze what is happening across the Enterprise providing accurate forecasts so that general management can adjust policies and call attention to problems that may affect the task managers and their costs. If general management is unsatisfied with how a task manager is performing or controlling costs against commitments, they should replace the manager, rather than try to edict some result.

It is not the intent of this book to discuss the principles of accounting systems. Instead I will examine some of the issues that influence the classification and management of cost, and the systems for providing visibility to this data, which can profoundly affect the success of projects and an Enterprise.

8.1 Purpose of the cost management information system

The cost management system function in today's business Enterprise is much more than an accounting system. It must fulfill several functions, including planning, forecasting, visibility at all levels of the enterprise, accurate cost accumulation, and proper distribution. The first is to provide a structure for accurately forecasting and recording the resources expended in *every activity* of the Enterprise. This includes not only the direct activities - - those labor and material costs expended directly on the products of the Enterprise, but also the effort expended in managing, marketing, keeping track of cost, the cost of acquiring and maintaining plant buildings, equipment and tools, travel, utilities, and even service to the community. Ideally, all of this data should reside in an integrated n -dimensional relational database that can be sorted through in any of the dimensions. This methodology will be discussed further in Section 8.3 of this chapter.

In our concept of integral management, the management of *all* costs is delegated to the level at which the associated work is delegated. We want the managers who are responsible for tasks to make cost tradeoff decisions to get their tasks done efficiently, and to be accountable for the results. For this to happen, first-line managers responsible for tasks must be able to create and negotiate time-phased resource expenditure plans for performing those tasks. When agreement has been reached, they must input the plans into the cost management data-base, authorize work-orders for proper accounting of the costs incurred, evaluate progress against those plans and re-plan the work when necessary. This requires on demand access to the resource expenditure plans and actual expenditures. It also requires the ability to modify the to go plan in a controlled manner. At the same time this access must not corrupt the integrity and the security of the database.

Attributes of an effective cost information management system include the following:

- It must provide a structure for estimating the cost of each product or service. Only then can the Enterprise set the price of those products or services

- It must provide for the accurate accumulation and display of actual costs to those responsible for meeting the budget, preferably with capability to generate earned-value data for evaluating progress against the planned schedule and cost.

- It must accurately distribute the costs of products, goods and services provided to customers to bill and collect in accordance with the terms and conditions of the sales agreement or contract.

- It should provide an integrated database of personnel and payroll data, maintain records of accounts receivable and payable, and provide for current and projected cash management.

2.0 It must provide a database of all income and expenses by product line, and for statutory purposes such as sales, payroll, property and income taxes, and reports to the shareholders etc. The historical database is especially useful

in looking at trends and estimating for new products or services.

8.2 Classes of cost

The cost of doing business can be described in terms of the direct cost of creating products, goods and services, and indirect
costs that are not directly relatable to the creation of the product, but are necessary in order to have the ability to make the
products. Typical indirect costs include management, cost of
money, facility costs (such as rent, furnishings, utilities and insurance,) and support personnel such as accounting, purchasing,
janitorial, and maintenance personnel, employee services and
benefits. These costs must be allocated in some fashion to each
of the products, goods and services. Good accounting practice
demands that these indirect costs be allocated to the products
on the basis of how much they use or benefit from these Enterprise functions. Direct and indirect costs are also broken down
by applicable resource type, e.g. labor of different classifications,
subcontracted effort, material, computers, tools, facility and
equipment costs, utilities, insurance and travel.

8.3 Cost/benefit correlation

The people who we would like to control costs in an Enterprise
are not in charge of overhead cost, which can often be equal to
or greater than direct cost. Many of the people who determine
the overhead or indirect cost neither control it nor understand it.
Moreover, their primary interest is in allocating those costs to
those who control the direct cost. Some of the issues in managing indirect cost are seen in the examples below:

1) A product division manager has little incentive to avoid
   spending overhead, thereby increasing the risk that they
   will fail in their assigned job, when that avoidance results
   in no cost saving to them. This is a fundamental reality,
   which undermines the premise that those who control

the direct cost can reduce the indirect cost over which they have little control.

2) A company that classifies much of its cost as overhead and deals with government entities on cost reimbursable contracts is at a disadvantage with other companies who have placed more costs in the direct category. In the former, management spends inordinate amounts of time on this subject.

3) If we are to control total cost, we must broaden the cost accountability of our management and ensure that actions are in place to minimize costs.

8.4 *Effective Control of Cost*

To effectively control cost we must put the true control of as much cost as possible in the hands of those who manage the direct base. The way to do that is first to maximize the functions that are direct and then to maximize the assignment of remaining indirect cost to the direct activity that benefits from it. If an individual is to be held accountable for controlling costs, four criteria must be met.

First, the individual must have the authority to make decisions that affect those costs. Second, that individual must have accurate visibility about the incurring of those costs. Third, no one else can have the ability to authorize changes to that commitment without renegotiating the basis with that accountable individual. Finally, the commitments made between that individual and his or her manager must be bilateral, not imposed.

Overhead costs have historically been a particular management problem, because in a sense, while everybody has them, nobody owns them. And while a single overhead rate has many advantages, it is improper if it prevents the majority of costs from being controlled, or properly allocated to benefiting activities. One favorite mistake of general management is to mandate overhead cost budgets when overhead expenses are too high for the direct base. This violates the concept of a contract, and is also ineffective in the long run. Smart managers know how to follow orders. Costs may meet the edict, but some critical function may be stopped in order to meet it, and general management will find this out later when some unpleasant manifestation of that decision shows up.

Another ineffective tactic in trying to control overhead cost is to focus on the salary and fringe benefit component of overhead. The result of this tactic is that these cuts are on the backs of the employees, and the resulting perception undermines trust. The reality is that employee fringe benefits *should* be the largest contributor to overhead and everything else should be minimized.

Overhead costs that are too high are a sign of a management failure at the top -- failure to assign responsibility and set reasonable expectations for those costs to someone who can do something about them. General management should develop guidelines based on valid bench marking of high performance parts of the Enterprise, get buy in from the rest of the management team, and then let them manage to those guidelines. Typically, these guidelines should be ratios of supervision to total employees, floor space per employee, etc. They may be set arbitrarily at first, but should be adjustable with experience to assure that they are realistic.

8.5 Knowing the Cost Influences and Delegating Them Down

Direct versus Indirect Cost

The determination of whether an activity should be direct or indirect has only three tests:

A. The cost of incurring the activity can be accurately and reasonably traced or assigned to the benefiting activity.

B. The activity that incurs the cost is one that the company is willing to have controlled by the benefiting organization or customer. An activity incurring cost sometimes needs to be indirect because it is a common administrative expense associated with the fiduciary responsibility to the shareholders/investors, or to all customers as a group, and the decision as to whether or not it will be an incurred cost cannot be left to any single customer relationship.

C. The volatility of the activity when fractionated to the benefiting activity level is acceptable to individual customers.

The following functions are strong candidates for direct charging:
- Program/product management
- Contract estimating/control systems
- Contracts
- Program-dedicated procurement/materiel
- Media services (reproduction and publishing)
- Program-related organizational training/development
- Program-specific marketing
- Program-dedicated facilities/equipment

- Computer service centers (CAD/CAM, scientific, etc.)

The following functions are candidates for direct charging through some sort of pooled work order or allocated prime cost:
- Functional management
- Central industrial accounting functions (financial analysis and support)
- Divisional subcontracts/materiel
- Operations/HR
- Divisional administration
- Divisional legal counsel
- Divisional business operations and marketing staff

The following are true indirect functions and overhead costs:
- Executive management
- Central finance
- General Procurement
- Small machines, desks, partitions, PCs under $10K, heat, light, power, water
- Employee fringe benefits

8.6 Managing Project Cost

Chapters 3 and 4 discussed the project planning process and the management roles and responsibilities for creating and negotiating the planned resources. They also discussed ownership by responsible managers for all the work to execute the plan. Here, we are concerned with providing the visibility into what is occurring during that execution to all levels of management in order to help them do their job.

Earned Value Performance Measurement

Managing project cost includes planning the expenditure of resources to accomplish the project work activities, measuring the actual resource expenditures, and the accomplishments those resources have produced, taking corrective actions when and where needed. This is known as an "Earned Value Accounting System and is required on major US government multi-year cost reimbursable contracts

I am a firm believer in the use of earned value measurement in the management of projects. There are those who argue that by monitoring schedule milestones, the need for an earned value system is obviated. I have found this is simply not true. By simply structuring the tasks to relate to meaningful and measurable milestones during the creation of the project plan, it is possible to use the resulting accomplishment measures to foresee problems long before the milestones themselves are missed and in time to take corrective action or to plan contingent action.

The key to doing this is a proper time phased database of the plan and a compatible and timely cost accumulation system. This data base is also used in combination with those of all other activities planned to occur in the Enterprise to forecast the pricing of those planned resources and identify the strategies needed to realize those pricing assumptions. This requires using the earned value system as the primary status and measurement tool to manage the project, not just as an adjunct.

One of the objections to earned value systems is that the Enterprise accounting system will not support earned value measurement. Today, with powerful personal computer spread sheet programs, this is no longer a valid argument, if the initial inputs are properly organized as we will see.
A second more valid complaint is that there are lots of bells and whistles in a formal government mandated system that are time

consuming and of questionable value. The approach I recommend works for projects large and small and is easily
mechanized. The outputs from the system are available monthly
by charge number but compatible with other Enterprise systems
such as Payroll, Billing, Overhead and space planning, etc. Most
important, it provides easy to display data for periodic project
status reviews at any level in graphic or digital data form.

The N-dimensional Resource Data Base
A key tool for managing project costs is a relational database in
which data can be viewed by any relevant set of categories. The
database begins with a work breakdown structure that includes a
box for every task required for that activity. Information must be
sortable by any of the dimensions. A work package is defined as
a measurable unit of work identified at least one level below the
lowest WBS level, with a measurable start and end event. Each
work package has a time phased plan tied to measurable master
schedule milestones. A resource ledger contains the time
phased resource plan with the same n-dimensions against which
actuals are measured. This database is the Budgeted Cost of
Work Scheduled, (BCWS). The budgeted cost of the effort actually accomplished is called Budgeted Cost of Work Performed
(BCWP).

Figure 8-1 illustrates the multidimensional nature of this database. The following discussion describes how this data is used
with the project cost performance measurement system. First
the plan is loaded into the data base. In each WBS box, the time-
phased resources for that element of work are described by performing organization and by resource classification. These
resources may be hours of various labor classifications, computer hours of various types, machine tools, material, subcontractor
effort, support services, office or shop space, special facilities
use, and so on.

Cost Account
Data Base Structure

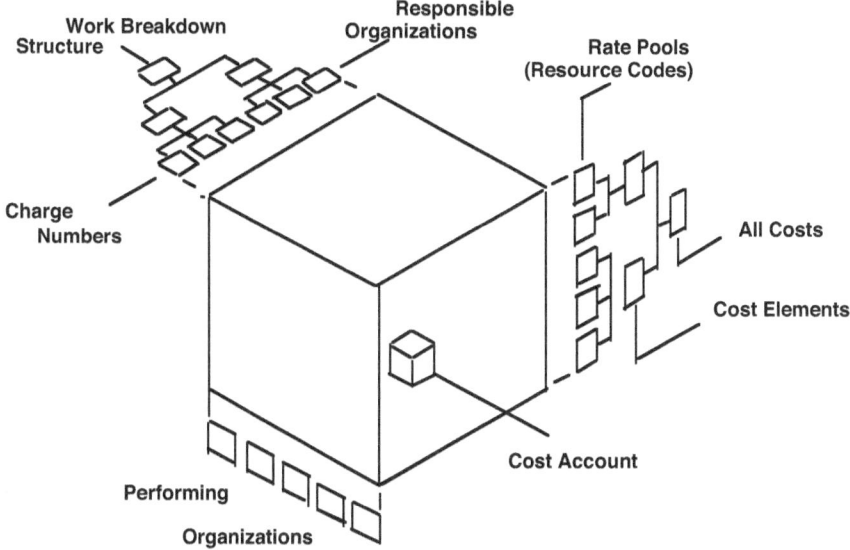

Fig. 8-1 The N-dimensional Cost Account Data

Forecast direct rates and burden are applied using applicable rate tables.

Forward pricing is important to forecasting these rates and burdens, that while a closely related subject, is discussed separately in Section 8.7.

Actual expenditures are accumulated each day or week, and the data base is updated weekly for labor, using actual payroll labor rates, and monthly for all other resources and burdens.

Block change control must be maintained over the time phased plan, with authority for change requiring multi-level security access keys to prevent unauthorized use or modification.

An example of an earned value performance measurement system is illustrated in figure 8-2.

A Project Earned Value
Cost Performance System

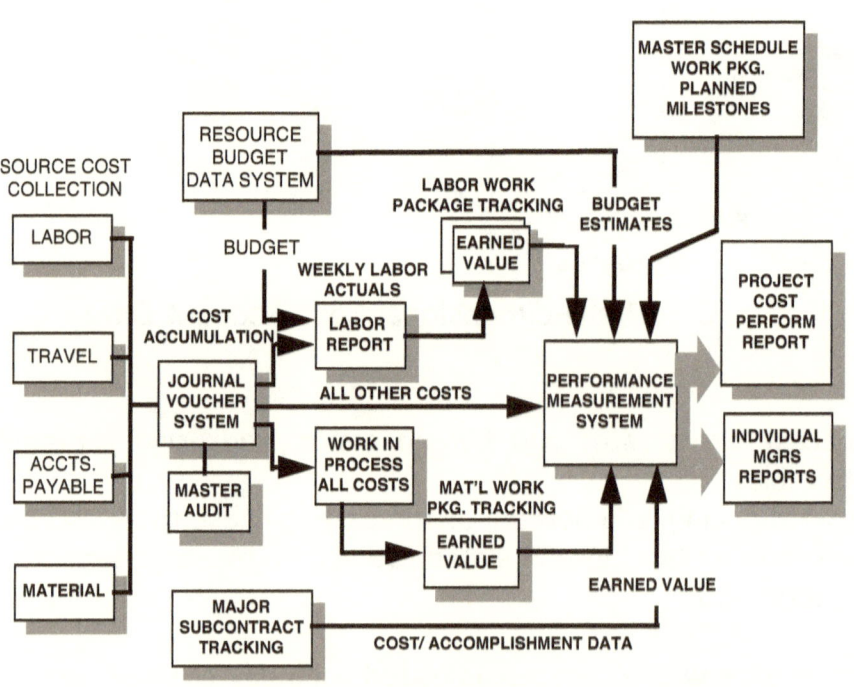

Figure 8-2 Example of an Earned Value Project
Cost and Schedule System

A project cost and schedule management system is an integrated set of tools consisting of a central data processing system
which operates on inputs from five resource data bases to generate all information necessary for monthly Cost Performance
Reports and their supporting data. This data processing system
integrates, sorts, computes, formats and summarizes the status
of every work package, and sums to create reports at any level
of the Work Breakdown

An earned value system can actually be implemented off line
even when the accounting system is not designed for it. An example of such an implementation using spread sheets is
illustrated in figure 8-3 and 8-4 though not filled out.

Budgeting 3T Work Sheet

WBS Element_____	FY 00											
Task & Resource	Oct	Nov	Dec	Jan	Feb	Mar	Apr	May	Jun	Jul	Aug	Sep
Program Milestones				△ PDR							CDR △	
Task Description & Milestone supported												
Time Phased Budget (BCWS)												
Equivalent Headcount												
Cum Equiv. Headcount	0	0	0	0	0	0	0	0	0	0	0	0
Labor Dollars												
Cum Labor Dollars	0	0	0	0	0	0	0	0	0	0	0	0
Subcontract Dollars												
Cum Subcontract Dollars	0	0	0	0	0	0	0	0	0	0	0	0
Materials												
Cum Material Dollars	0	0	0	0	0	0	0	0	0	0	0	0
Other Direct Charges												
Cum Other Direct Charges	0	0	0	0	0	0	0	0	0	0	0	0
Total DollarBudget	0	0	0	0	0	0	0	0	0	0	0	0
Cum Total Budget		0	0	0	0	0	0	0	0	0	0	0
Actuals (ACWP)												
Equivalent Headcount (hrs/160)												
Cum Equiv. Headcount												
Actual Labor Dollars												
Cum Labor Dollars												
Subcontract Dollars												
Cum Subcontract Dollars												
Material Dollars												
Cum Material Dollars												
Other Direct Charges												
Cum Other Direct Charges												
Total Dollar Actuals												
Cum Total Dollar Actuals												

Figure 8-3 Earned Value Spread Sheet Part 1

The time phased resource plan is the budgeted cost of work scheduled or BCWS. The spread sheet is shown in two parts. They are little more than typical three T charts (Task, Time, Talent) that are required in some form for planning and inputting expenditure plans to accomplish the tasks with time. This chart is for a single work package or set of tasks that support a project milestone, in this case two design review milestones, and shows the number of people needed each month and what type they are at least in terms of their rate of pay and overhead burden rate.

Earned Value Determination

WBS Element_____	FY 00											
Task & Resource	Oct	Nov	Dec	Jan	Feb	Mar	Apr	May	Jun	Jul	Aug	Sep
Program Milestones				△ PDR							CDR △	
Task Description & Milestone supported												
Work Accomlished (BCWP)												
Budgeted Equivalent Heads Claimed												
Cum Labor Hrs. Claimed												
Budgeted Labor Dollars Claimed												
Cum Labor Dollars Claimed												
Budgeted Sobcontract Dollars Claimed												
Cum Subcontract Dollars Claimed												
Budgeted Material Dollars Claimed												
Cum Material Dollars Claimed												
Budgeted Other Direct Charges Claimed												
Cum Other Direct Charges Claimed												
Total Work Earned This Month												
Cum Total Work Earned to Date												
Cost Variance (BCWP-ACWP)												
Labor Variance												
Sub Contract Variance												
Material Variance												
Total Cost Variance Cum to Date												
Schedule Variance (BCWS-BCWP)												
Labor												
Subcontract												
Material												
Other Direct Charge												
Total Sched. Variance Cum to Date												
Basis of Measurement of Accomplish												

Figure 8-4 Second Half of Earned Value Spread Sheet

. It also has provisions for other resources required such as materials computers, etc. The chart also provides for filling in the actual expenditures or actual cost of work performed (ACWP) by resource type as they occur and are recorded in the accounting system.

Figure 8-4 is a continuation of the spread sheet that provides for the read out of accomplishment. Figure 8-4 captures the budgeted cost of work performed (BCWP) which is simply the planned resources for that task or set of tasks, but which can only be claimed when the meaningful and measurable event has occurred. Algorithms can be established for intermediate measures of accomplishment between measurable events, such as design documents released into the configuration management system as a percentage of the current total estimated documents required. However, since these algorithms are surrogate for the meaningful measure which in the example shown is satisfactory completion of the critical design review for example, I personally would not allow more than 75% of the total accomplishment to be claimed until the actual completion milestone was met.

Accountants seem to like this data displayed in tabular form for the current period only. I prefer to see the data in graphical form as illustrated in the following figures so that recent history and trends are readily visible. This is accomplished by providing visibility to prior data for at least the last six months and future plans for the next six months.

Figure 8-5 shows one typical output from an earned value cost performance measurement system at any level of the WBS that meets this objective. The difference between BCWS and BCWP is the schedule variance, which can be measured either in time or dollars and the difference between BCWP and ACWP is cost variance.

Sample Earned Value Performance Measurement System Output Chart

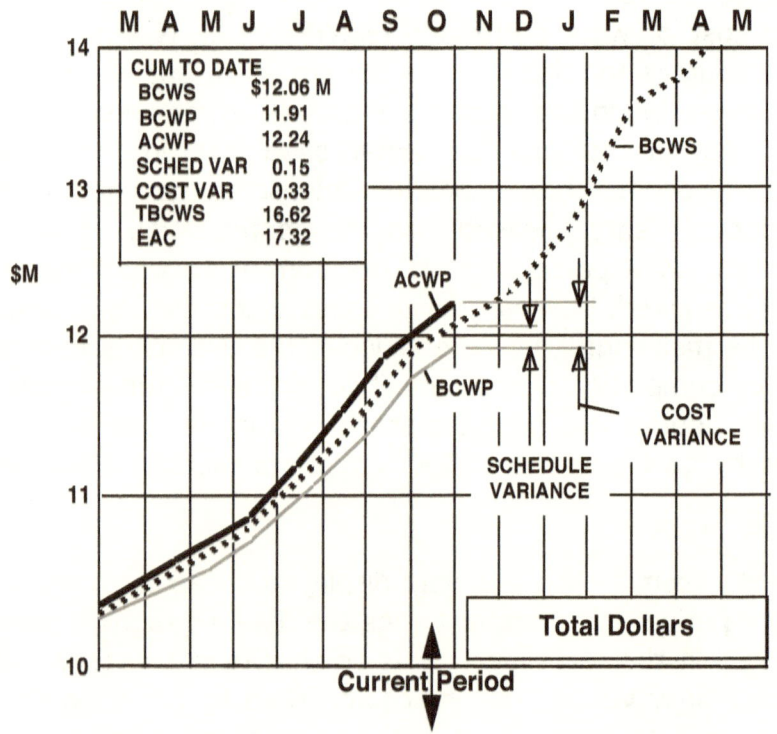

Fig. 8-5 Earned Value System Output Example

. There are three things to be noticed in examining this chart. First, if you were to look just at Budget (BCWS) compared to actual cost (ACWP) as a simple cost accounting system would, you would conclude that the activity shown was $180K over budget at the end of October. Second, by including the actual accomplishment (BCWP), it becomes quickly obvious that the real variance is worse by almost a factor of two ($330K).

The third point is that while the total budget (TBCWS) for this activity -- which ends beyond the time window of this chart -- is $16.62 Million, the responsible manager is projecting that the actual cost at completion (his estimate at completion or EAC) is $17.32M for a variance of $700K. What that manager is saying is that he or she expects that no corrective action
will improve either the cost or schedule performance between the current period and completion.

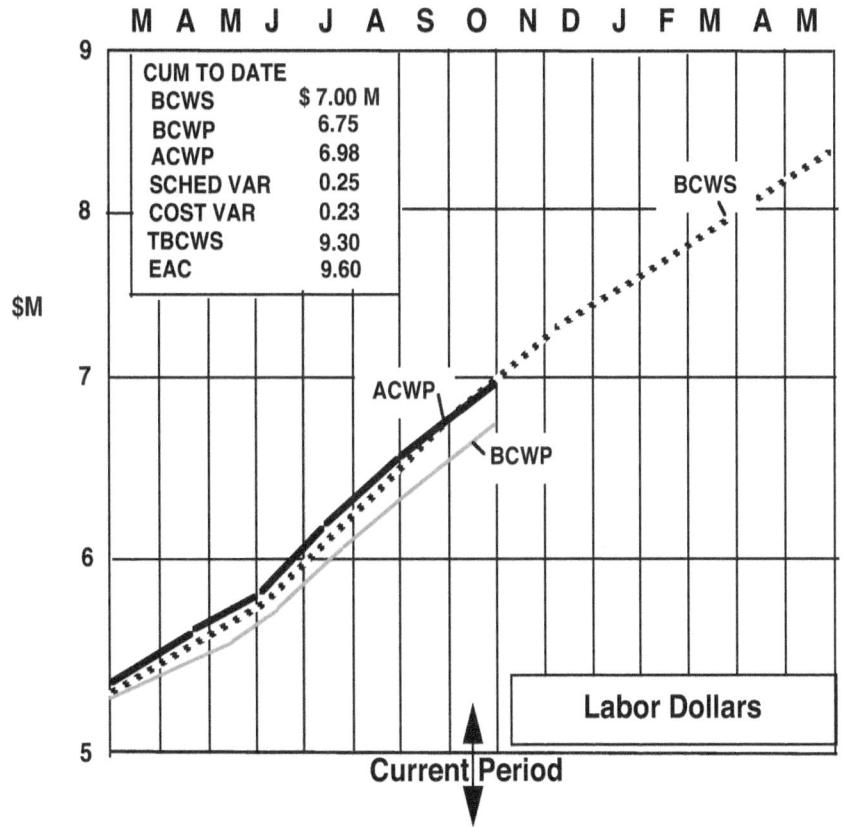

CUM TO DATE

BCWS	$ 7.00 M
BCWP	6.75
ACWP	6.98
SCHED VAR	0.25
COST VAR	0.23
TBCWS	9.30
EAC	9.60

Figure 8-6 Labor Report

In projects with which I was associated, these data were reviewed in a monthly program cost status review, summarized by
responsible segment or WBS manager. The boxes contain the
digital data for precision, and the analog data gives a feel for
what is happening with time.

Figures 8-6 through 8-8, also available from the data break down
the overall cost data of figure 8-5 into labor and non-labor components. We can see in figure 8-6 that while the labor
expenditures are right on plan, the work accomplished is more
than a month or $250K behind schedule. The responsible man-
ager is not expecting this condition to worsen.

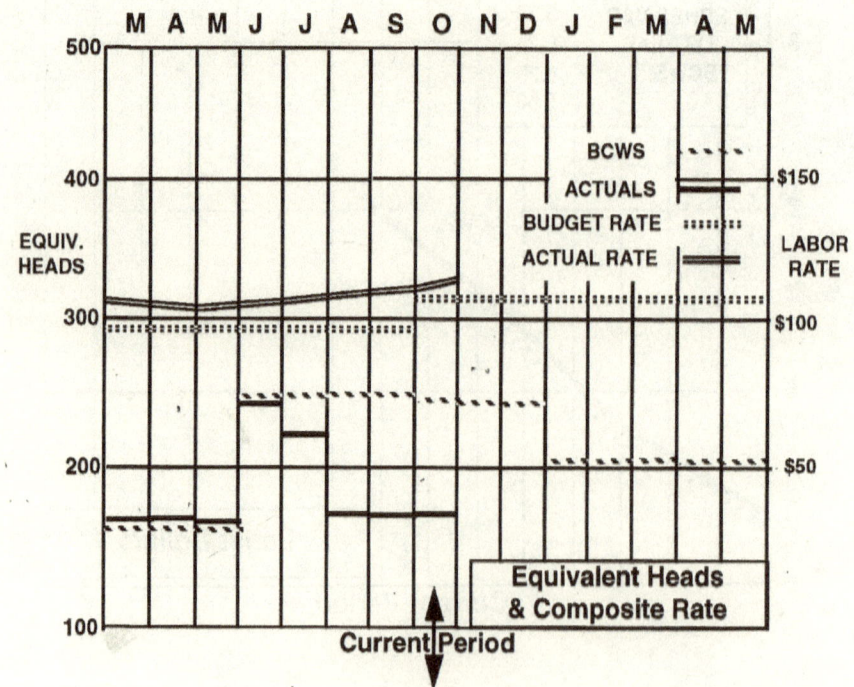

Figure 8-7 Equivalent Heads and Composite Rates

Figure 8-7 provides the data that shows where the labor problem has been. In fact, the number of people working in the activity is less than planned, but the composite labor rate -- the actual direct labor rate plus burdens -- has been consistently higher than planned.

Looking then at figure 8-8, we can see that the non-labor costs of this activity are higher than planned, but the accomplishment is actually ahead of schedule.

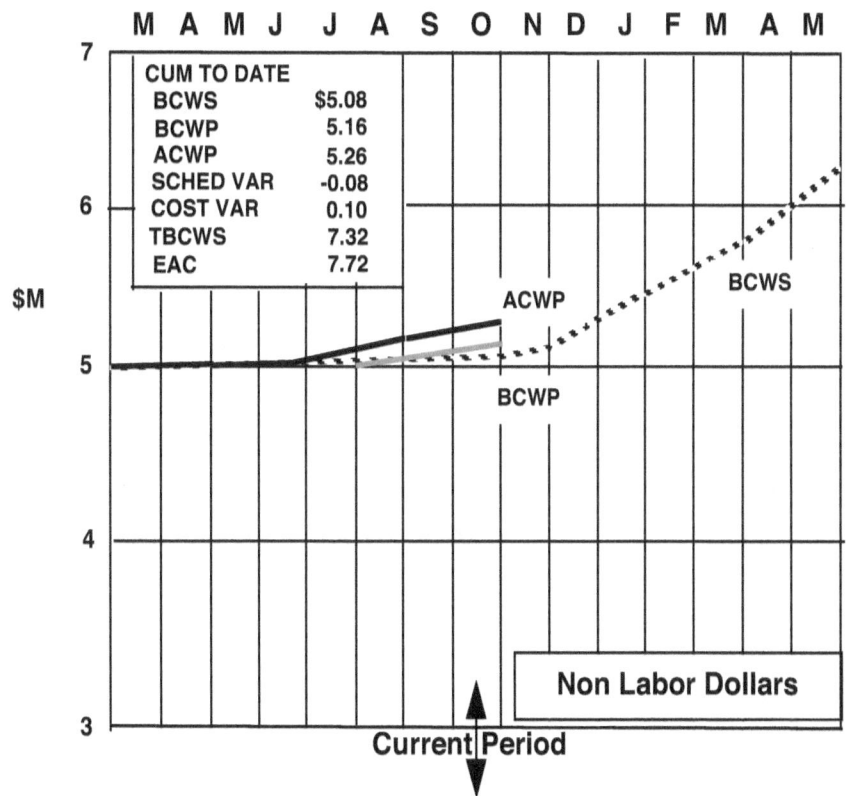

CUM TO DATE	
BCWS	$5.08
BCWP	5.16
ACWP	5.26
SCHED VAR	-0.08
COST VAR	0.10
TBCWS	7.32
EAC	7.72

Figure 8-8 Non Labor Report

8.7 Forecasts and accountability

It should be clear that care in the planning and estimating of the resources needed to do a set of tasks that make up each work package is an important ingredient in the project budgeting process. Similarly, it is important to be able to forecast labor and overhead rates, considering business volume, and its effects on those rates. This forecasting relies on the soundness of all the project plans in the Enterprise, but integrates them as part of the Enterprise governance as a whole.

8.8 Computers, Buildings and Machines

Computing equipment and software cost is another area that has for some reason confounded management. No one can do anything without a computer anymore. Computers of various types and capacity have become so ubiquitous that it is hard to imagine productivity without them.

New Technology Distorts Traditional Equipment Accounting

I worked for a company that structured its accounting system many years ago with the direct labor as the unit of work to be burdened to equitably distribute overhead cost. This made eminent sense in that the largest elements of overhead cost were in fact labor related. Employee benefits, workspace, human resources cost, general and administrative expense such as the cost of management are primarily related to the cost of labor. At the same time, the cost of fixed asset equipment such as machine tools, office machines for reproduction and data processing were purchased or leased and their amortized cost was treated as a part of overhead cost and distributed across the direct labor base that used them. This also generally made sense since all these devices were operated by people who charged their time to some work authorization.

But then came the microprocessor, and with it came computer-controlled machine tools, automated processes for manufacturing, testing, and even design, CAD/CAM and flexible machining centers. These items cost more and more and did more and more with less and less direct human participation. Often the machinist's main role is to program the machine and set up the work pieces, and sometimes not even that. There are probably more labor hours spent on equipment maintenance than on producing product.

The same thing has taken place in the fabrication and assembly of electronics. Surface mount technology is largely automated from the circuit layout to final assembly. This includes, not only the multi-layer printed wire boards that components are mounted to, but also the very highly integrated circuit devices that can be made by a foundry to your design with only a set of design rules.

Implications on Costing of Equipment

Now if we take this trend to its extreme, we have a very expensive machine shop with many grand computer controlled multi-axis machines with automated raw stock delivery and loading and one machinist who mainly checks to see if things are working properly. In the electronics shop, the same thing is going on, as the design is directly translated from computer aided design data to printed wire boards with all steps automated including test. Then the parts are placed directly from tape fed inventory and wave soldered or bonded again without human intervention. One electronics technician watches to see that nothing is going amok. Does it now make any sense that the machines are an overhead cost spread against the labor hours of that single machinist or technician? Of course not! First of all, we would have an infinite overhead rate. Second there would be little relationship of cost to benefiting job. In fact the traditional roles have now been reversed. It is the machines that are doing the direct job, and the technician is spread over all jobs in the shop and should be overhead.

What happens if these expensive beauties sit idle? If you bought them, you can't just get rid of them. To dismantle and sell them you might get 10 cents on the dollar even if they are brand new. Unless you can sell their use to outside buyers, they get charged to overhead where they may take five years to write off.

The decision to buy these kinds of facilities must be connected to the specific business need that will use them. More over the execution of the job that requires them must be planned to account for the lead-time of acquiring and bringing these facilities on line *after the job is in hand.* The amortization plan and the return on investment of those specific facilities must be accountable by the project manager to that job and not spread over all of the rest of the business unless actually used by the rest of the business.

This was not the case in my company at the time. Over-optimistic managers convinced general management to make these investments on the come, and the work never materialized or disappeared. The result was an unmitigated disaster -- not once, but repeated several times. It also happened with large mainframe computers. These acquisitions which were now on the books sat idle, saddling the rest of the decreased business with an overhead cost that could not be eliminated. *And no one was held accountable.* Ironically, these same managers later complained that the cost of manufacturing in house was too expensive and non-competitive, and all manufacturing should be out-sourced.

What are the implications here? The productivity of machines and equipment has become a dominant cost element of the product and must be part of the direct cost base, not an allocated cost. This has led to the concept of "activity based accounting".

8.9 Activity Based Accounting

This approach requires a performing activity to account for all its costs including equipment and apply them only to the work going through that activity. In other words, it requires treating machines and facilities costs just as labor costs have traditionally been treated. This method can be applied to the investment in machine tools and special use facilities. It should connect investment strategy directly to new projects. Just as you don't hire workers before you have the work for them to do, you shouldn't invest in specialized equipment and facilities until the work is in hand. Using this approach, you plan the initial phases of new work that will require new equipment or facilities in order to recognize the lead time to procure and bring them on line, and to plan for interim solutions at the time the project is approved.

More than 10 years ago, the Harvard Business School Press published an important book entitled *Cost Management for Today's Advanced Manufacturing*[6]. This book presented a conceptual design for a new cost management system -- the work of a consortium of successful industrial corporations, academia, professional accounting firms, and government agencies. This group

---

[6] *Cost Management for Today's Advanced Manufacturing the CAM-1 Conceptual Design*
Edited by Callie Berliner and James Brimson Harvard Business School Press 1988

was created to develop a new cost management paradigm to address the needs of the computer integrated manufacturing techniques coming into wide use. One of the strong themes of this international group was that Activity-based Accounting was a crucial part of any cost management system in the contemporary manufacturing environment. The idea is that costs are incurred by activities that are naturally and easily identified by all members of the organization.

Activities are easy to relate cost and performance to, if one identifies *all* the resources used in the activity. Activity-based accounting also minimizes the amount of and mysteries associated with allocated costs such as overhead. Since investment in facilities and capital equipment can also be related to the activities that require them, management can establish a clear cost benefit relationship and measurement system. In short, activity-based accounting is responsive to the problems we have discussed in this chapter, and yet, ten years later, many Enterprises have yet to implement this type of cost management approach. Read the book.

8.10 Stability, Instability, and Unanticipated Events

One of the vagaries of the financial vernacular is the idea of fixed or uncontrollable costs. There are really few if any fixed costs. Debt service and certain vested employee benefits such as retirement plans are fixed costs because a long term obligation exists, but even here, their actual annual cost may vary with investment yields and interest rates. Some costs are more difficult and take longer to affect than others, but very few are fixed. The equipment we discussed earlier in Section 8.8 is an example of what some would call a fixed cost at least until those facilities were fully depreciated, or written off against profit.

When people or facilities are not being used for direct work, they must charge to something often called lost productive time or idle time. Some level of idle time is required to avoid the cost of firing and hiring, but if that level is exceeded for any length of time in an area of the Enterprise, it raises a red flag that requires corrective action. Jobs do get cancelled unexpectedly, and business that was anticipated may not materialize. Prompt response to these events is imperative, and it is a function of the management control system to provide visibility to these effects quickly.

A Case of What You See Ain't Necessarily What You Get!

One of the fads of the 1990's was "outsourcing" of many functions -- most often services, and in some cases entire manufacturing functions. In the period starting about 1990, several large companies, plagued with rising and seemingly uncontrollable costs of data processing, were lured into outsourcing this function in its entirety.

Corporate directors of information services seduced by this siren song espoused by management consultants sold all their information systems equipment and software for management information systems and the large host main frames used for technical data processing to a firm that specialized in providing data processing services. These providers, had built up a market and reputation doing this work for small and medium sized businesses that lacked the expertise to build their own management information systems. They were ready, willing, and able to expand their markets.

What They Saw

These service providers would provide the same services to companies who wanted to rid themselves of this "problem". They would handle payroll, cost accounting and mainframe technical host computing while shouldering the additional procurements, maintenance costs and so on. This would all be done on a fixed price 10-year basis. According to the numbers run by the consultants this was cost-effective compared to what these companies were spending to perform the function in-house.

What They Got

Several of these companies, on the recommendation of their IMS directors and consultants, took this step without considering the ramifications of a downturn in business. That down-turn in business in fact occurred across a large segment of industry and they found themselves saddled with a multi-year fixed cost for computational services that they could not use and still had to pay for. Now *that's* a fixed cost! More important to us is that it surely wasn't effective cost management. The decision-makers violated one of our principles of project management. Frequently ask "what if?"

Changes in market conditions and other effects on business volume must be considered when making cost decisions. This is just one example of how business volume instabilities can affect cost management decisions.

Since computing is such a fun cost management subject, I thought it worth a chapter devoted to managing this particular resource. Chapter 9 explores some observations and ideas on this subject.

8.11 Contract Roles and Forms

In any business transaction, there is explicitly or implicitly a contract. Whether you are buying or selling, you will be party to a purchase or sales contract. The nature of that agreement may have a lot to do with how your cost accounting system will be used for that work and what the implications are of costs exceeding estimates. Chapter 12 discusses contract forms and their applications, but it should be noted once again that in the concept of integral management, even transactions between organizations within the Enterprise deserve contracts. Therefore contract types should be of interest to every manager, not just those who are responsible for sales or buying from suppliers.

Chapter 9 Managing Computers

9.0 Purpose

This chapter examines the acquisition, management and accounting of computers in today's competitive environment.
Business, particularly business involving the development of
complex products and technology, has seen dramatic growth in
the volume and importance of computing resources in almost
every facet of the Enterprise. Managers with vision recognized
the opportunities for increased productivity, and the technical
workforce pushed for more computer resources even where the
management did not see the handwriting on the wall. Whether
managers liked it or not, the voracious appetite for distributed
computing changed the face of business information systems.
This explosive growth, coupled with the computers lightning-like
obsolescence, has made this element of the cost of doing business a major management challenge.

9.1   Background

In 1980, with the emergence of powerful small computers known
as then as "minis" like the DEC VAX series, many companies
found themselves with an inconsistent application of their accounting practices because they were classifying computers by
their size, rather than their capabilities. In an attempt to fix this
problem, many companies chose to treat all computers like mill-
ing machines and charge them into overhead. This simplified the
accounting problem but created fundamental management problems that plagued these companies for the next fifteen years.

For those who chose this approach, this decision removed scientific computing costs from the direct contract cost base and put
them into overhead at a time when these costs were burgeoning
in response to the requirements of their work. The immediate

effect was to reduce the direct base and increase the overhead to be allocated. The next effect was for senior management to expend far too much of its time trying to micro-manage the cost of these resources because no one other than general management had ownership of them. This was destined to fail.

It was assumed that if computer cost was budgeted as controllable overhead, management of this cost could be delegated to burden center managers. In fact, the cost of computing spiraled upward in spite of a great deal of management attention, and for good reasons.

In government contracts, ever-increasing customer specifications dictate how software must be developed, how computer modeling will be done, often with the requirements to deliver software in a specific format or higher-order language, or for use on a specific host machine. There are also ever-increasing customer requirements on security that preclude the sharing of facilities and operating systems between programs. These are unique to programs, not to services or agencies. The result is a tendency to preclude the efficient sharing of computer resources even though the government requires its suppliers to demonstrate a credible benefit received vs. cost incurred relationship on individual contracts as well as in the aggregate.

9.2   *The Computation Demands of Today's Business*

Complex computational effort is an integral and growing part of the development of complex products. It is accordingly a growing element of the cost of fulfilling the *work* and closely coupled to the ability to do the work.

Increasingly, all work involves the creation and management of information. In my business, for example, this was typified by the signal *and* data processing of surveillance, target acquisition and recognition sensors, and the use of this data either onboard a sensor platform (such as a satellite) or remotely. This trend continues with the great increase in graphics in real-time simulation and multimedia presentations, so we can expect to see still more rapid growth in computing requirements.

It is not possible to estimate or negotiate the cost, nor to implement the work on a project without knowing what computer tools will be used to support those tasks. During the conduct of the work there are tradeoffs between the use of computer resources and personnel, and often between conducting tests and computer modeling, and always between the type of computer resources and programming cost.

Charging computing to overhead, as many companies do, prevents the proper tradeoffs, and moreover, in some cases does not properly distribute the cost to the benefiting effort. Budgeting the cost of computing equipment from the top down ignores the real linkage between the job and tools required. General management cannot manage computing any more than it can specify how many hours it takes to write a program or run a test. General management is therefore forced to make Solomonic decisions between needs...and frankly, is doomed to do a lousy job of it.

When computers are part of overhead, prudent lower levels of management, who use computers efficiently and make the tough cost-benefit tradeoffs, recognize that they pay for the waste of the sloppy manager anyway. They are therefore incentivized to make maximum use of overhead to reduce their direct cost and contract risk.

9.3 A Better Approach

The answer is not top-down management, but rather the delegation of responsibility down to the same level in the organization that we delegate people management. I believe that computers should be budgeted and accounted for as if they were people as shown in Figure 9-1.

Computers as Employees

The fundamental concept behind this proposal is that in most businesses, computers are like direct employees. We therefore should manage them, plan for and account for them just like people. Computers are model employees. They take direction well, they do the tasks requested, and generally follow directions faithfully. They have good memories, and help reduce work for others, but sometimes get sick. They faithfully maintain time-keeping records. They can even have an employee number.

Computer Management

When we hire an employee, it is on the basis of a planned need with an expected time-span. If the predicted work does not occur, we do not adjust the rate of the employee upward while the employee works fewer hours. We charge that employee's time to lost productive time until we can find another assignment. If none can be found, the employee is laid off.

Proposed Pricing Approach

Before acquisition, for the specific application, the cost-recovery strategy must be established.

A. <u>Dedicated Computers</u>. Dedicated computers are those computers that are used only for a single project, or are imbedded, such as a simulator or test equipment, or are required by

COMPUTER	SALARIED EMPLOYEE
* Amortized acquisition-cost based on useful life and depreciation strategy	Annual salary
* Ownership Cost	Administrative support costs
* Operating cost	
* Maintenance & repair	Medical care and benefits
* Improvements/upgrades	Education, training & promotion
* Cost of unsold time due to less than expected utilization	Lost productive time
* Planned utilization over which cost is spread to establish rate	Standard work week over which cost is spread to establish rate
* Direct rate per hour	Rate per operating unit

Figure 9-1 Computer Labor Cost Analogy

security to be isolated. This type of computer should be treated as either a piece of special contract equipment. Or, if its life is greater than the application, its yearly cost can be recovered fully by simply dividing the yearly cost by standard shift time or calendar time for weekly billing.

There is no lost productive time, and the contract using the computer pays all of the cost regardless of utilization, since the equipment is not available for other use.

B. Multiple-use Machines. These are to be used primarily on one project but several tasks and available for other users some of the time. For these the basis for "full employment" of the computer should be established. An example might be 1.5 shifts five days per week with 10% lost productive time and 1.5 shifts for maintenance or growth.

Costs for the pool should be established for amortized acquisition cost in $/yr. planned depreciation; cost of ownership including maintenance and repair, operation, utilities, software fees, etc. and the amount of lost productive time that is reasonable for overhead planning.

C. Rate Stability. Computers would not be re-priced upward retroactively, but would charge to overhead when not productively employed. If overhead charges exceeded reasonable levels, management would be expected to "surplus" the computer. If usage went above the plan, the benefits of the effective lower cost per unit could be retroactively priced, or used to adjust the prospective price. Computer acquisition would be tied to the proposal strategy for new business and on the basis of direct cost minimization for ongoing contract effort. Managers would not go buy computers before they were needed. They would be incentivized to share when the work load allowed it so that their direct costs on contract would be lower.

The key, in short, is to present the manager with a direct tradeoff under his or her control. He is the one that proposes the work,
justifies, negotiates it with the customer and is later measured on his performance in getting the work done within cost.

9.4 Implementation

Data System Requirements

It has been suggested that new systems must be developed in order to charge computers direct. I would argue that the problem can be quickly solved with a duplicate of existing labor accounting system using the analogies of Figure 9.1. Any enterprise labor cost accounting systems, if adapted for computers, can obviously handle as many computers as there are employees, and account for them properly to contract, overhead, or whatever. Suppose we wanted to direct-charge ALL computers—even PC's. Computers that have a clock could certainly have a job log and billing algorithm. Those that don't could have a time card filled out by users and signed by the responsible supervisor just like an employee's timecard.

What to Do Before The Work Arrives.

What do you do with people before the work is there? Computers can be handled in the same way. They all get charged to overhead (lost productive time). Remember, everyone has to be somewhere.

Chapter 10 Communications

ORGANIZATIONAL AND PROGRAM PROBLEMS CAN OFTEN BE TRACED TO COMMUNICATION FAILURES. WITHOUT CLEAR COMMUNICATION OF EXPECTATIONS, THE EMPLOYEE (OR MANAGER) WILL DO ONE OF THREE THINGS:
- *WHAT THEY THINK YOU WANT DONE;*
- *WHAT THEY WANT TO DO;*
- *NOTHING!*

10.0 Introduction

Most defeats in battle and in business can be traced to communication failures. People work better when they understand what is expected of them; this is as true of the relationship between employees and managers as it is of people on a project team. Expectations must be communicated clearly and should be mutually understood. The communication channels must remain open so that if there are problems in fulfilling a plan, they can be aired and dealt with.

10.1 Effective Communication - A Keystone of Successful Management

All management, be it project and/or enterprise management depends on clear communications. The most modern and up to date communication technology or media may not necessarily insure effective communication.

Cartoons on the walls of employees' work areas can be revealing. Once I was walking through a plant, and passed by a cubicle where a man was working. A large cartoon was tacked to the wall above his desk, which read: " Management treats me like a mushroom. They keep me in the dark and feed me sterile chicken

_____!" Now here was an individual who felt he was not getting communicated with!

What are the objectives of communication within an Enterprise, and what are some of the approaches that are effective in achieving those objectives?

Communication engenders trust if it is frank. Employees in any Enterprise are bombarded by rumors. E-mail broadcast capability provides a very efficient and rapid medium for spreading them. It also provides an effective soapbox for anyone to air a griev-ance or perceived wrong. If Enterprise management does not communicate to its employees regularly and effectively, the ru-mors and grievances are the primary input they have.

Enterprise management can and should provide substantive in-formation on how the place is doing, what problems are to be faced, what good work deserves recognition, and what the lead-ership sees on the horizon about a year ahead, that might affect employment. I believe that during business down turns, man-agement should share its objectives, expectations, and actions taken to maintain equity between the management structure and employment levels as an example. In short, if you want em-ployees to act like they are part of the team, then treat them like they are part of the team.

Project Management communication has somewhat different ob-jectives aimed at coordinating project related activities. For instance:

- Formulation and coordination of definition and planning - setting directions

- Dissemination and maintenance of authoritative refer-ence for the objectives, ground rules, definitions, contractual agreements -both internal and external,

- Coordination of changes to the baseline plan, assessing progress and reacting to problems.

10.2 Effective Methods of Project Communication

A. Project Management Memos

Chapter 7 discussed the purpose of these memos in integrating and coordinating a project. An example of a project management memo format is shown in appendix 1, which was used to initiate the design to unit production cost process.

Note that there is a title and section reference. There is a purpose and/or objective stated. There is an action and responsibility statement for each affected organization, and finally there is a budget statement. Signature blocks exist for all affected organizations and the project manager, whose signature issues the memo. The document requires coordination and buy in.

B. A Program Requirements Manual

The concept of the Program Requirements Manual is discussed in detail in chapter 7. It is a dynamic compendium of all program requirements, the program management memos, program plans and decisions to provide a road map of the entire project.

C. Status Meetings

Project status meetings where all project activity leaders are represented are very effective means to review progress, technical assessments, and cost performance. Generally held weekly by the project management, this venue also provides a forum for discussing problems, upcoming events, and reactions to the data presented. As mentioned in prior chapters, they are not problem solving meetings, but rather problem identification and progress evaluation meetings. With today's video conferencing capability, these meetings can encompass widely geographically separate participation, saving immense amounts of travel time and money.

D. Team Meetings

Integrated product team meetings are similar meetings held to discuss status and, in this case collaborate on problems and solutions among the team's project responsibilities. The frequency may vary and may be daily if necessary.

10.3 Effective Enterprise Management Communications

A. Staff Meetings

Weekly Staff meetings at all levels of an enterprise are a very important communication tool, provided they accurately pass on the messages both downward and upward in the enterprise. The ability to hear about concerns, decisions, events, impending changes, and to respond or ask questions in real time facilitates prompt and more accurate dissemination in both upward and downward directions. They should be mandatory even if very brief.

B. Status Overview Meetings

Projects should report status to senior management monthly in most cases, and tp Enterprise management at least quarterly to keep them informed--not to get "helped". General management should set time aside for these meetings. Not only is it important that the front office know about problems in the event of queries from outside, but they should be hearing it from the project first. It is also a good way for Enterprise general management to show its support and interest in the project.

C. Occasional all Supervision Mtgs. with Enterprise Performance and outlook presentations

Enterprise general management should hold occasional meetings with all supervision to share the performance and outlook for the Enterprise. Generally, this should include one at year-end when the years performance can be put in context and the expectations for the coming year honestly predicted. Whether good news or bad, it needs to be shared so employees know what to expect. Sometimes these projections will turn out to be off, but if the Enterprise management shared its best estimates, that will be appreciated. A portion of the meeting after presentations should be devoted to Q and A. One caution on these meetings is to assure no insider disclosures or data that has not been disclosed per SEC regulations.

It may be prudent to hold other such meetings as a result of special events or development that will affect the work force.

D. Newsletters

Letters from the Enterprise leader are useful when key events occur such as reorganizations, key personnel promotions, or when a major problem occurs that gets media coverage. This gives the boss the opportunity to give a first-hand picture to employees, quickly and clearly.

Regular newsletters have never appealed to me, because a) they have no news, and b) they create a work force to publish them and fill them when there is no news. On the other hand, when there is something to report, it is a good tool to have and employee interest stories help to maintain a team atmosphere. Perhaps today, Enterprise e-mail fulfills this need better.

E. Getting out in the trenches

There is nothing more effective in connecting with employees, than getting out in their work areas and taking an interest in what they are doing. It is one of those things you can't do enough of. When their leaders show that they care, everyone feels better about what they do.

10.4 Individual Communication

A. Personal Objectives

I personally believe that every employee from top to bottom of the Enterprise should sit down with their supervisor, discuss expectations and establish written measurable objectives for the coming period of performance. This is a powerful communication tool if it is practiced with diligence. Since it takes a lot of supervisors' time, it often is sloughed off or done in a half-assed fashion. If done properly, it makes performance reviews a great deal easier.

B. Individual Performance Reviews

Honest and perceptive performance reviews provide important feedback to both employee and supervisor if they are conducted in conjunction with personal objectives.

C. Recognition Awards and Bonuses

Money talks, and so does public recognition of achievements. They should not be cheapened by misusing or overuse. I prefer team awards for achievement, because most achievements are from teams, and it sends a good message.

10.5 Computers No Substitute for Face to Face Meetings and Printed Material.

What goes out over the Ethernet is often lost in the ether.

Broadcasting data or program decisions is often ineffective. This seems to be because so much e-mail is copying others, it ends up like junk mail, and dilutes the important data. Retention is also poor. Archiving can help, but that requires discipline on the part of the receiver. The fallacy of the paperless society is that it generates more paper, not less.

10.6 Coordination Tricks, Stalls, and Countermeasures

I found over the years that some people avoid buy in on decisions by simply failing to act and sign off on a coordinated document. Sometimes a subordinate of the affected manager simply keeps it circulating for comments. It is often an attempt at a pocket veto. Another ploy is not to come to the coordination meetings or the negotiating table. The solution to this problem was simple enough. If a key player failed to attend or send a representative to a coordination meeting, the results of the meeting were documented and distributed. A time limit was established and announced by which if there was no response, that manager's failure to respond would be noted and taken as tacit approval.

10.7 Setting Objectives and Expectations

It is important for managers and employees alike to set objectives and state their expectations in a receptive way. It is very helpful in establishing an effective basis of job satisfaction and performance. This subject, which as we said earlier is important in both directions is discussed in chapter 14.

10.8 Feedback and Evaluation

Feedback and job evaluation is much easier when objectives have been discussed and acted on. When someone does a great job on an assignment, acknowledgement of that and public recognition is a great way to get continued high performance.

Performance appraisals are very sensitive subjects, and must be done fairly and objectively for all those who report to you. It is easier to do if there has been a good discussion of objectives and expectations at the start of the review period. This subject is discussed further in chapter 14.

10.9 Compensation and Incentives as Aids to Communication of Objectives

A very effective way of communicating objectives, setting expectations, giving feedback on the results, and rewarding excellence is through the use of financial incentives.

Employee Incentives

It has long been a practice to incent senior managers on business unit performance and other objectives through the use of performance incentive bonuses, and stock options as part of their compensation plan. Bonuses have also been widely used to reward outstanding performance at all levels of employment. But, relatively few businesses have used profit sharing as a means of rewarding the employees for their efforts in achieving an unusually profitable year, for instance. Those companies that do it seem to enjoy excellent labor relations and feel that this sharing enhances the Enterprise performance. This is not an easy program to get started in an Enterprise, but I believe it offers a great opportunity to get work force involvement in productivity improvements, cost savings, and better management labor relations. It really says, "you are members of the team."

Incentive Contracts with Suppliers and Customers

What works for people also works well for business relationships. Contract incentives are a particularly interesting subject that is discussed in depth in chapter 12.

10.10 Quality of Communication

It is not enough to communicate. It is important that the quality of the communication be good enough to get the desired message through to the desired recipient.

Meetings and Formats

While meetings are excellent opportunities to communicate, they however have a tendency to be either solely top down or up. I have always felt that in most meetings, discussion should be encouraged and relevant opinions solicited. Meetings should be structured, but informal enough that constructive discussion can take place when appropriate. The leader can loosen the atmosphere so that subordinate managers will not be afraid that their bosses don't want to hear from them.

Status meetings should have a structured agenda where the news is presented, but to avoid someone shaping the news, questioning and constructive feedback of reaction to the presentations followed by discussion tends to prevent that shaping. The worst thing the senior management in the meeting can do is sit there like a bump on a log and not react when they see something exemplary or disturbing. At the same time, such meetings are not the place to solve problems, but rather to identify them and assign action if none is underway.

Some Pitfalls to Avoid

1. I have always been comfortable with give and take in meetings, but many people are not comfortable with that. It must also be recognized that some bosses don't appreciate having their agenda disrupted in a public forum. I have made this mistake more than once. If you sense that situation in a meeting environment, you have to arrange one on one discussion to present your view.

2. Some people try to use a large meeting as a forum to argue their agenda that you know is wrong, and you can get sucked into this kind of trap if you aren't careful. A meeting with a large audience is not the best place to pursue an argument, even if you know you are right. Some wise sage offered the following advice:

NEVER WRESTLE WITH A PIG. YOU BOTH GET DIRTY AND THE PIG LIKES IT.

COROLLARY: NEVER ARGUE WITH AN IDIOT. SPECTATORS MAY NOT DISCERN WHO IS WHO.

I have to admit that I violated this advice more than once, and I remember each of them with embarrassment. It's better to just murmur "incredible!" and you'll feel better. (See item B below for clarification)

Potentially Useful Tongue in Cheek Concepts

A. The Veracity Factor - A Concept for Evaluating Communication

Many years ago, as a new program manager, I chanced to be in the audience for an erudite presentation. I observed that several speakers as well as some of the critics in the audience exhibited, in varying degrees, some compelling characteristics. As the presentation progressed, with give and take from the audience, I became increasingly aware that what I saw and heard could be categorized and evaluated by use of solid engineering principles. This led to the formulation of a powerful communication evaluation concept: The *Veracity Factor.*

The concept can be used to evaluate the content of presentations -- and audience reaction for that matter. This veracity factor or index is a density function having the units of bullshit per cubic mouthful.

The numerator is universal, being measured in terms of volume or mass. The units of the denominator -- cubic mouthfuls -- is less known, but is the standard cubic mouthful, or Herman. I am told that Herman is encased under glass at Versailles near the silver metric standard.

Now, there is an interesting but somewhat esoteric facet of the veracity factor. The units are analogous to the reciprocal of signal to noise ratio. Having been a guidance and controls systems engineer, I noted that if you advise someone (who generally doesn't have a clue) exhibiting a 'high veracity factor' that he or she has a high one, *they will very often go proudly telling others that you said so.* Thus, the application of the veracity factor tends to be self-regulating.

B. The Stamp - Prompt Feedback

Another tool I have seen employed for immediate but inhumane critique is the rubber **BULLSHIT** stamp. Most effective for presentations using an overhead projection of vu-foils, when you can no longer endure a presentation with very high noise to signal, is to go over to the projector and apply the stamp in real time. I guarantee it will bring things to a halt. Of course, there are drawbacks, and it isn't really in the spirit of this book.

C. Alternative Usage

You probably shouldn't use the rubber stamp on your boss or any other individual who may have direct influence over your future employment -- even if you are sure that it applies. In this or similar circumstance, one alternative is to murmur "Incredible!" at the appropriate point.

10.11 Summing Up

Communication is one of the biggest challenges of effective management. It isn't easy, and sometimes it seems that the message just doesn't get through. The bottom line is that no news is bad news in the operation of an Enterprise or a project, or any relationship for that matter. So, good communication is worth the effort, no matter how much effort it is. And don't feed the troops fertilizer. You are always being rated.

Now that we have explored a few of the issues of communication, we will move on in the next chapter to look at ways of communicating and dealing with those who do not necessarily share the values we have described in this book.

Chapter 11 Dealing with Other Styles

11.0 Background

I am often asked, "how can you instill and practice an integral management style in an existing environment that is so much less than your ideal?" "What if your bosses, customers or competitors don't share these values?"

We know there are people in all walks of life that do not concern themselves with fairness, honesty, and integrity. So not everyone plays by the same golden rules. Many business environments are politically driven, not performance driven. Self-serving behavior is often rewarded. It seems everyone must compromise their standards to survive in this competitive dog eat dog environment.

I urge you not to succumb to that thinking. Our concept of Integral management does not imply naiveté, getting walked on, or turning the other cheek. This chapter discusses how high integrity managers protect against unscrupulous, opportunistic, unlucky or just plain stupid behavior.

11.1 Different Cultures Inside the enterprise

Like society, business enterprises need standards of behavior to discourage unproductive behavior. Unfortunately, there are many in the world with 'win lose' philosophies that must be dealt with. They have other rules: *Win at any price; He who has the gold makes the rules; I win, you must lose; What's mine is mine and what's yours is negotiable; Or, It doesn't matter what the goal is or if it is met, it is the game that counts.* It's safe to assume that self-interest rules their actions. Some of these people are likely to work in your enterprise.

Suppose you are in an organization that is not in tune with the principles of 'integral' management we have discussed. What are some of the actions you can take to build an environment of trust?

11.2 Meeting the challenge

If you are a manager at any level and instill this expectation within your circle of influence or control, its success doesn't depend on the external world or even the rest of the Enterprise outside of your control operating with the same philosophy. One just has to recognize what that larger environment really is, and be wary of its foibles. By your actions or inaction, you alone set the standard for those who report to you.

You can begin building trust within the circle of your influence, by practicing and expecting integrity in every aspect of that area of influence. You set the standard, dis-incent and discourage behavior that doesn't meet that standard. If people don't live up to that standard after being counseled, you weed them out, remembering that no matter what it writes or says, *management demonstrates its true intent by what behavior is rewarded and tolerated.*

At the same time, you do your best to shield those who work with you or for you from the aberrations caused by any lack of integrity outside your influence. Even if you fail to succeed in maintaining that buffer, if you have earnestly tried, those who depend on your integrity will appreciate and respond to it. Others outside your influence will begin to see that result and be affected by it in their dealings with your group.

Is this easy? No way! It is hard work to earn and maintain trust in the work place. There are many conflicting pressures and the job never ends. But the dividends are tremendous if you are willing to work at it and have the courage of your convictions.

11.3 Effective Transaction Management

As a general rule, it is wise to assume that no one you deal with adheres to the principles of integrity we have discussed. Good business arrangements and contracts make no assumptions about ideals, but set expectations and provide definition of necessary performance by both sides with provisions in the event of default by either party.

The Concept of Dental Equilibrium

Quite a few years ago, I had the opportunity to attend an executive program in business administration at Columbia Graduate School of Business in Harriman NY. One of the very able professors on the faculty of that program was Dr. Boris Yavitz, then dean of the Graduate School of Business. Among the many subjects he discussed was a concept he called *Dental Equilibrium*. As I recall it, this concept went roughly as follows:

You have to go to the dentist to have some work done. You know it isn't going to be your favorite experience.

You sit down in the dentist's chair and the assistant puts on your bib and assembles dangerous looking paraphernalia to be used in your treatment. Then the dentist comes in, picks up and tests his drill. As he stands poised and asks you to open wide, you reach over and gently but firmly grasp him -- by the scrotum--and say, "Now, we're not going to hurt each other, are we?"

Dental Equilibrium.....the essence of deterrence, is a surrogate for a very important concept – the balance of power in all facets of business, both outside and inside the organization in which you work. It is the basis of contracts that we will discuss when we get to chapter 12.

Face all the Issues of the Transaction

Don't avoid controversial or unpleasant issues when establishing a business relationship. Use tact, but don't avoid facing them. Document the transaction with a written contract. Frank, hard negotiations --well documented -- make for good mind melds, or at least help to uncover irreconcilable differences before it is too late. The resulting documentation later also serves to correct any memory or integrity lapses of the parties, their heirs and assigns.

Create arrangements that incentivize desired behavior and disincent self-serving, dishonest, or non-productive behavior at others expense. Partnerships are great, but it takes common mores of both parties to make it work. Sometimes, you don't find out that you each see things differently until much later in the transaction. It is best for business transactions to assume that people are no damn good, and then hope that you are wrong. The method for doing this in the beginning is a contract. Formal contracts and their various forms are discussed in the next chapter.

Document performance and any other issues that occur during the conduct of the contracted job, to assure that there is a trail that shows that your actions met the contract. You would be amazed how many disputes are lost because of poor documentation of actions taken during the course of the work.

Remember that deterring undesired behavior by either party requires a balance of power in the transaction. Look for win -win solutions, but if dealing with a win lose oriented adversary, always be prepared to street fight and win. That means that you must have equal power. If there must be a fight, be prepared for some china to get broken.

Transactions Within the Enterprise

Within your enterprise, a contract about a transaction can be quite informal, such as a simple task statement, a drawing, a need date, and a charge number to use. When I went to work in the aerospace business, there was a method that was called an **ANVO**. "ANVO" was an acronym for "*Accept no verbal orders.*" I don't know where these originated, but it was a half page note format with "ANVO" across the top, and "To" and "From" space, and these were readily available with a piece of carbon paper to provide a ready copy. They were used to document a transaction, or inform of an action or problem. Simple, quick, effective. As far as I know, they may still be used, although most now are sent by e-mail, which has its pitfalls as discussed in an earlier chapter.

If Deterrence Fails

Occasionally one party will not honor the terms of an agreement. As often as not, that party will accuse the other of violating the contract. The importance of maintaining good records that show compliance becomes really clear when this happens. So what do you do?

When deterrence fails, threats are worthless. Action is the next step. You must decide whether you are willing to see it through to the finish. Most people aren't. Negotiations can begin effectively only when your transgressor recognizes that he or she cannot win. If you are going to fold when it gets tough, save yourself a lot of time and money and roll over in the beginning. I have watched again and again where half hearted measures have been substituted for decisive response -- usually based on perceived financial trade-offs. It's a losing strategy, and it marks you as a patsy for more transgressions. If your adversary believes you will take decisive and painful action in response to the transgression, they are much less likely to transgress. The ability to inflict serious pain only deters if the will to employ it exists. Having the moral high ground is necessary but isn't enough. You must have the cards to play as well, and be willing to play them, with finesse, of course. Avoid knee jerk and premature response. Carefully pick your strategy and the arena and then act decisively. Dr. Yavitz phrased it simply. *If you have to fight, go for the jugular.*

11.4 Unilateral Direction and its Pitfalls

A contract--whatever its form-- is a bi-lateral document requiring agreement by both parties. By definition, it cannot be imposed by one party on another. Unilateral direction is something else: a command, an order, or a demand, and the issuer must take the responsibility for all the consequences of that action.

Unilateral direction has a place, particularly in a life and property threatening crisis, where sometimes snap decisions are needed and the leadership must take the responsibility and tell people what to do, but not very often. The director is making the assumption that he or she has all the relevant data and is required to give the direction, in the interest of expediency or safety.

Unilateral direction is often used by leaders with low integrity and low self-worth. It is a way of wielding power over subordinates who cannot easily defend themselves. This type of leader generally does not take the responsibility for the result of that direction unless it turns out well. But then those types take credit for everything good and none of the bad that happens, anyway. If that direction is accepted even though disagreed with, the recipient has become a potential scapegoat if bad things happen. Beware of this type of person. If you believe you are being told to do something wrong and or damaging, at least ask for the direction in writing. It forces the issuer of that direction to consider the consequences of a written directive.

The receiving party of unilateral direction, has some choices: First they can accept the direction. Second, if they disagree with the order, they can refuse, creating a confrontation in which if the issuer has the authority, can lead to a charge of insubordination. The recipient needs to be on firm ground indeed to choose this option. Third, the recipient can accept the order, but demand that it be put in writing (one use of the ANVO), or finally, they can pretend to accept the direction and then covertly avoid doing so.

Clearly the last option is the safest out for the recipient of an order that he or she believes is wrong, but the consequences of this can be devastating. Talk about undermining trust. It also may cause a disaster, if the action was assumed to have been taken, and, of course it destroys the credibility of both the order giver, and the recipient. You can see that buy-in is an important, but unlikely step in unilateral direction. One might conclude then, that giving unilateral orders is not a very good idea. In a high integrity environment, edicts are very rarely used. Contracts on the other hand, whether implicit or explicit, engender trust, communication, and buy-in. Use them in some form within the Enterprise, as well as outside.

11.5 Ethics and Ethics Programs.

It always fascinates me to hear people start talking about teaching business ethics. I read something not long ago about a retired military officer who makes his living as a consultant teaching ethics to heads of corporations. He probably makes a lot of money at it, too. But what does this suggest? Did these people who are running large corporations have no ethics before he came along? Were there no standards or expectations clearly put forth for behavior?

Written Codes of Ethical Behavior

Is a code of ethics a good idea for an Enterprise? I think it probably is because, if properly done, it is a way of communicating expectations. But if you have one, you must follow it in every way with *all* stakeholders of your enterprise. Otherwise, it is worse than having no written standards. Unfortunately, many companies fail in this regard, so the code becomes meaningless.

The Rush to create Ethics Programs

In 1987 a Blue Ribbon panel chaired by former Deputy Defense Secretary David Packard investigating over-runs and waste, in defense acquisitions concluded that in addition to problems within DoD, that industry needed to strengthen its own policies and procedures. In response the National Defense Industry Association issued the National Defense Industry Initiative on Business Ethics & Conduct.[7] The result was that programs were established at all major defense companies focusing on three actions. First, a promulgation of-the company's declared ethics and standards; Second, a mandatory program established to train all employees on the implications of these standards, with advice and discussion of Video case studies to illustrate dilemmas and how to deal with them; Third, an anonymous hot line established where anyone who had an ethical problem or wished any inappropriate behavior that they witnessed could report it. And so, almost immediately, the cottage industry of ethics program consultants and trainers was born. Rules were developed and promulgated to assure that everyone acted ethically.

---

[7] https://www.dii.org/about/dii-principles

What's wrong with this picture? First, it suggests that the problem was primarily at the lower levels and there was where the training was needed, which was the tactful thing to tell leaders, but not a valid assessment. Second, if you believe that the leaders set the climate in an Enterprise you might conclude people who were well educated with lots of business experience but no ethical values could become leaders of corporations -- and there is some evidence that supports that conclusion. Another possibility, is that people who grew up with ethical values did not see them as applicable in the work environment. In fact, there is a considerable body of evidence going back at least to the beginnings of the industrial revolution that supports this thesis. Reading the history of the industrial revolution in the US and England, and the emergence of the "Robber Barons" and the labor movement offers testimony to this point.

This line of reasoning suggests, that ethics were (and are) not highly valued in business management. Greed, power, and self-aggrandizement seemed to drive the behavior of many individuals. Over the years, anti-trust and fair labor laws, cost accounting standards, and federal acquisition regulations (FARs) all came into being to put end to abuses that stemmed from this attitude. So, embrace whatever thesis you like, as now comes a new politically correct program called Business ethics. I doubt that the Packard commission envisioned what ensued.

The Unanticipated Results of Ethics Programs

Did this program instill a new environment of trust? No indeed! In fact, in companies that enjoyed reputations for high integrity, ethical behavior, and employee trust, it actually undermined trust. Investigations were initiated on the basis of anonymous phone calls etc. Crazy things happened. I saw one instance where questionnaires were sent out to all employees asking if they had ever been asked to mis-charge their time, or had ever heard of any instance where someone else thought they had been asked to do so. Does that sound like a chapter out of the McCarthy hearings of the early 50's? I received a poignant note from a long-time employee who received one of these question-naires, in which he said " This doesn't sound like the company I have known and respected." Right on, brother!

In companies that suffered from lack of ethical values, the pro-grams were seen as a whitewash of real problems. In both types of companies, the anonymous hot lines soon came to get used by disgruntled employees or those being laid off in a business recession as retribution against their supervisors and managers. Mischarging and Sexual harassment were two favorite charges used for this purpose. Another favorite was the accusation of shipping defective products. Investigators were dispatched on what can only be described as witch-hunts based on these anon-ymous accusations. The result was a kangaroo court where the object of the complaint had no rights, could not confront an anonymous accuser, and was assumed guilty by overzealous in-vestigators. Did this encourage managers to make the right decisions on personnel actions? Not likely. It undermined the in-dividual managers' decisions, and was seen by them as a lose-lose situation. In short, like so many crusades, the so-called Eth-ics programs spawned grossly unethical behavior.

Ethics Defined

Rules cannot be defined for ethics. Ethics are the values that guide behavior in the *absence* of rules. What are they? I believe that ethics are defined by how we expect others to behave with respect to us and vice versa. Fundamentally, the golden rule. If you don't have integrity as a fundamental environment, you cannot create a program of ethics enforcement. If you do have an environment of integrity, expectations are clear, and no "program" is needed. That integrity must be present in all facets of the business.

What if the ethics of companies were in fact the same as the ethics we hopefully learn from parents, educators, and religious leaders instead of Wall Street or Business schools? Would management labor relations be based on distrust? Would greed rule? Would we need to teach ethics to chief executives? I think not.

Ethics and the Integral Manager

There is an old axiom that states: *Power corrupts!* I fear that there is more to this axiom than we would like. I would modify the statement, however, to: *Those who thirst for power tend to be easily corrupted by it.* Those who advance their cause at the expense of others and succeed, are or become predators.

Predators stalk the unsuspecting and those they perceive as weak. When they run out of ready prey, they turn on each other and even their own offspring. If that weren't bad enough, they attract scavengers who find their nourishment in the detritus of battle. These creatures don't care who wins, only that the leavings are available. This symbiosis creates the toadies who serve the predators. In an environment that tolerates this predatory behavior, these scavengers in turn become the petty bureaucrats, who for lack of any other ability promote the latest fad. Not a pleasant environment in which to work every day.

This is why I believe it is so important for senior managers to have and set high personal ethical standards, and to apply the same standards in the work environment. They must demonstrate every day that power has not corrupted them, and that they merit the trust, meet the highest standards of integrity even in the face of enormous pressures. That is why they get paid the big bucks.

11.6 Situational Ethics

The foregoing discussion raises a thorny issue called situational ethics.

In dealing with one another, with customers and suppliers, personal ethics should apply equally well. But what does one do when personal norms cannot apply? For example, our personal ethics say that killing another is wrong, yet during war, we are called upon to kill or be killed. What is different? Expectations! In warfare, we are presumably fighting for some high purpose, and it is the duty of those who take the oath to fight to do so. It is understood that the enemy is trying to kill you, and vice versa. Victory demands destruction or surrender of the vanquished. There is only one ethic that governs "civilized" war. That is that the vanquished be given a choice. But until the battle has been decided, the expectation is that each side is trying to destroy the other.

In business, the pressures of competition can put enormous stress on a company's ethics. Sometimes this competition is construed to be a war. Competition is a crucible where integrity gets tested, and often broken. But business is not a war.

Frequent Flier Miles

Here is a question to ponder. Most of us are familiar with frequent flyer awards that are used by airlines to encourage patronage of their airline. The more you fly, the more award miles you win. These go into your personal frequent flyer account. Now, suppose your travel is occurring as a result of your business, and the cost of your travel is properly billed as a direct cost to a customer. Are the frequent flyer miles you earned in that travel, which are useful for free future trips, yours? The airlines have provided no way to credit anyone but you personally with those awards.

Now consider a different situation. A person responsible for purchasing commodities is offered money by a supplier to buy that supplier's products. These supplies are used in the creation of products that the buyer's company sells to its customers. If the money paid to the buyer were used to reduce the cost of the supplies, it would be a discount. If the buyer personally received the money, it would be what is commonly known as a kick back -- an unethical and usually illegal act.

So, the question is this: Should one use the frequent flyer miles to pay for future business trips on behalf of the customer who paid for the prior trips that earned the award miles?

Dealing with Foreign Sales and Cultures

As American business interests have expanded internationally, they have encountered the dilemma of cultural differences in business dealings. In many other countries, practices considered anathema in the US are the norm and within the law. In country agents, facilitators, and consultants are part of the infrastructure used by those countries to practice commerce. While US laws preclude such roles in government procurements, paid lobbyists routinely work Capitol Hill and influence legislation. Yet, those lawmakers passed legislation requiring US companies to abide by US standards when doing business in other countries. It is difficult to know whether these laws are being adhered to, but the legislation clearly puts US companies at a disadvantage when competing with other nations' companies in international markets within the laws of those countries.

I suggested earlier that ethics are based on expectations about behavior in any situation. Assuming the practices are legal in the country where such practices occur, one might ask whether our policy is valid.

The questions posed in these two situations are difficult. They both make me uneasy for widely different reasons. I personally would feel more comfortable about frequent flyer awards if they could only be used for upgrades and preferred treatment to reward our patronage. I also wonder about the wisdom of imposing our standards on other cultures when we are not quite congruent ourselves

11.7 Coming to Grips with Management Fads

Some are born to fadism. Others have fads thrust upon them. Fads are often embraced by bureaucrats, casting about for some way to make a mark. This is how it has always been. But with the ever-increasing clout of the investment community behind them, management fads have become insidious.

A Study by the National Research Council

A book published by the National Academy Press entitled *Enhancing Organizational Performance* documents a Study by the NRC that examined among many other issues, the manner in which organizations respond to their rapidly changing environment. This book is worth reading and its conclusions regarding the introduction of untested innovations as a
management response to problems struck a responsive chord with me.

In my view, ethical integral management neither depends on nor seriously responds to fads from business schools, Wall Street analysts, or management consultants. Effective management relies on common sense principles evolved and proven by long term success, but which have in recent times been lost in the fog of bottom line pressures. I am repeatedly amazed at how uncommon this common sense has become in the upper reaches of major corporations. Somehow, under the pressures, egos get warped along with perception of truth and people lose track of fundamentals driven by ambition, adversity ...or the Peter Principle.

Fads Fade Fast, but the Malady Lingers On
Reality eventually overwhelms a fad. The half-life of a fad is about two to three years at most, often less. The damage from a bad innovation, however, can last a decade. It can also be terminal. Quite often these faddish actions are taken belatedly after finally recognizing a long ignored management problem. Had senior management been more diligent in setting realistic expectations and realistically measuring results, the enterprise could have prospered even in adverse conditions. By looking to the fad of the day, it is possible to create a perception of corrective action rather than address the root cause of a problem. Often the beneficiaries of the temporary perceptions of enhanced results have been a few senior executives and the investment community who take the money and run, leaving a hollow shell in their wake.

Dealing with Fads
The Bear Hug strategy
Embrace the fad. Clasp it to your bosom. Keep doing what you think is right and dress it in fads clothing. Everybody wins. The faddist feels accomplishment and you keep doing what you knew to be right. This approach requires the rationalization of situational ethics in order not to get sick to your stomach, but it works. The only downside, is that the faddist, instead of being ground in the dust of defeat as you might prefer, goes on to bigger and better fads. The solace in this is that you can tag

that party with the veracity factor and feel better while muttering "incredible" occasionally.

Ride out or Run

Unfortunately, some of these "innovative strategies" are bigger than you can deal with. You can register your concern, but often no one wants to hear, and you can be viewed as resistive to change. Then, you have to decide whether to grit your teeth and ride it out, minimizing the damage where you can, or disassociate yourself from the strategy and leave that enterprise. Here, your personal integrity is your best guide. Can you continue to do your job or not? Remember the half-life is generally two years or less.

11.8 Conclusions

Since maintaining high integrity is hard work, one must gauge the result of their efforts in the larger Enterprise recognizing the foregoing discussion. The rewards of a high integrity environment are reduced stress and increased job satisfaction. On the other hand, if you judge that your endeavors and principles are not valued by the leaders of your Enterprise, you must at some point ask yourself whether this is a place you want to continue your career. Otherwise you are in for frustrating times.

Each time I read this chapter I am uneasy. I have a reputation as an honest pragmatic manager, but I am also an idealist, and have been accused of tilting windmills on more than one occasion. As I analyze my feelings, I suppose that having set forth principles that I believe in for managing with high integrity, I fear that this chapter tends to belie them. Yet, that is not what I want to convey.   The principles of integral management are proven by success, and depend on having that mix of idealism and pragmatism in about the right proportions. By and large, the issues discussed in this chapter should not exist. Unfortunately, they are typically part of the landscape. In my ideal, they would not be there, but they happen, and can't be ignored.

So as we leave this subject, I propose that the integral manager who engenders trust is *idealistic* enough to have the faith in those who will share the vision of high integrity; *pragmatic* enough to recognize those who do not share that vision; *courageous* enough to make changes needed to ensure success while resisting those changes that are specious or embraced to hide failure; and *wise* enough to tell which is which.

Chapter 12 Contracts

12.0 General

What is a contract? Simply stated, it is a mechanism for two parties to define what each will get out of a transaction within mutually agreed constraints.

There are many forms of business arrangements for contracting for goods and services of any kind of Enterprise. If you are in business, you contract with customers to sell your goods and services. In order to sell them, you purchase other supplies, raw materials, sub-assemblies and services of one kind or another from suppliers. All of these require some agreement and understanding by both buyer and seller as to what will be supplied, by when, and what the buyer will pay to get them. This description, and all the understandings between the parties, become a contract when the parties put their signatures on it.

Contracts can take many forms with different characteristics that are applicable in different situations. I have had the opportunity to enter into many contracts -- both as a buyer and a seller -- with individuals, governments, and commercial businesses. They range from verbal agreements sealed with a handshake to contracts for $5 billion worth of work to take place over a period of eight years and defined by a stack of paper that would fill a room.

12.1 A Seemingly Dry but Vital Subject

I cannot overemphasize the importance of this part of your business activity and how often it is fouled up in practice. It sounds like a straightforward problem to work and one that an attorney is trained to do. Wrong! Attorneys are often very knowledgeable about standard clauses, (of which there are too many). They are well versed in the case decisions that affect or change the interpretation of those clauses, but they are not necessarily equipped to create the body of a contract that is unique to the product or task. In this sense there are good contracts people who are lawyers, but lawyers are not necessarily good contracts experts. In many cases the best contract expert may be the specialist who is going to do the actual work contracted for. Legal jargon generally obscures the intent of the contracting parties, and insures future work for the attorney. The best arrangement is to have the project engineer and an attorney work together to define the contract. None of the foregoing should be taken as a recommendation for the Enterprise attorney or their staff not to review every contract. That careful review is a vital part of the system of checks and balances.

With all the expertise and brilliance and best of intentions, there is no way to write a perfect contract, All things cannot be foreseen. You try to anticipate what could happen, and lawyers can be of considerable help in this area, but there is no such thing as a bulletproof contract.

One time about 25 years ago I was a member of a team finalizing a large ($2.5 billion) complex contract. When we got all finished and about ready to execute, we and our customer added a special provision at the end which stated, *"None of the foregoing shall prevent the use of reason and logic."*

Now, you can just imagine how the lawyers on both sides reacted to that! They would not let those words be used in the body of the contract. Yet, that is exactly what we wanted to be understood. In the end, we compromised. The words came out of the contract body, and we inserted a preamble that said, *"None of what follows in this contract shall prevent the use of reason and logic ".* The lawyers begrudged us that because it wasn't technically part of the contract. But it made the point we wanted to make to all those who would use that thick contract as a guide for what they were supposed to do, and those on the buyer side who would evaluate what was being done. *Don't do or let anyone else do something stupid because the contract says to. Take it up with the other party if you think it is wrong.*

12.2 Definitions

A contract is a documentation of the intent and expectations of two parties about a transaction between them. It must be clearly stated so that it *faithfully records a meeting of the minds of the two parties.* This is where most contracts fail. A contract defines what is being purchased and what the consideration or payment is in return. It also defines the terms and conditions under which the contract is executed. When must the product be delivered? Does it have to perform some function in order to be acceptable? When and to whom must payment be made? When does ownership transfer? Are there conditions on how the work must be done? Is there a warranty or guarantee? What if the buyer has a change of mind during the process?

Defining the Job -- the Work Breakdown Structure (WBS)

As part of defining the work to be done, it is helpful to create a diagram of the total job similar to a table of organization. This chart, which is called a work breakdown structure, defines every element of work deemed necessary. The WBS is generally organized by deliverable products and or services, with the activities needed to create them as sub-elements under those products.

The WBS with its dictionary (which is akin to the charter that goes with each block on a table of organization) is a framework for assuring that nothing has been forgotten, and therefore defines the contract statement of work. It also provides a structure for costing each element of work for the contract. A simplified example of a WBS is included and discussed in Chapter 7.

The Test of Definition

Good contracts are negotiated agreements, not unilateral directives. Negotiations help the contracting parties to understand each other's intentions and objectives. What do words such as "shall", "will", and "ensure" mean? A contract signed without understanding the implication of every word included and every word omitted in it is a potential time bomb. Your signature, unless obtained under duress, says you agree with everything in the contract.

In writing a contract, no matter how trusting and honorable the relationship, each party must assume that the other party will disappear shortly after the contract is signed and before the contracted work is done, and therefore two other people, who had no idea of what was agreed to or why, will have to complete the transaction based on what was written down. It should also be assumed that these other people may be dishonest and will take advantage of every ambiguity to avoid holding up their end of the bargain. These assumptions, by the way, are not theoretical. People do die or move on to other jobs. Companies change hands and the new party may have different mores than the party you shook hands with.

12.3 Matching the Contract to the Job.

The purpose of this section is to examine what types of contracts are appropriate to what kinds of activities. We will start with the simplest. Contracts become more complex as unknowns associated with the product (and therefore risk) increase. Also, in the case of contracts that require product development, the client may wish to structure the contract to balance such factors as performance and cost.

Simplest Types of Contracts

A. Firm Fixed Price (FFP): A purchase order is placed for a catalog item at a catalog price. This requires no disclosure by the seller of the cost of the goods. The market sets the price.

This type of contract is the simplest form of a Fixed Price Contract. Note the conditions: A well-defined off-the-shelf item with no unknowns. Figure 12-1 illustrates the cost-profit relationship for this kind of contract. It should be noted, however that the seller has only to commit to the price, and the buyer has no knowledge of or interest in the actual cost in this type of contract.

If the job is to deliver components that meet a certain specification, the seller should and will cut every corner possible while meeting the minimum requirement of the letter of the contract. Federal Acquisition Regulations specify a default provision for fixed price contracts where if the seller defaults, the buyer can go hire a replacement contractor to complete the work at the first seller's expense.

It should be clear that the seller earns the maximum profit by doing the job at the absolute minimum cost. In this contract form, the old adage that a dollar saved is a dollar earned is precisely correct.

Profit vs. Contract Cost
Firm Fixed Price

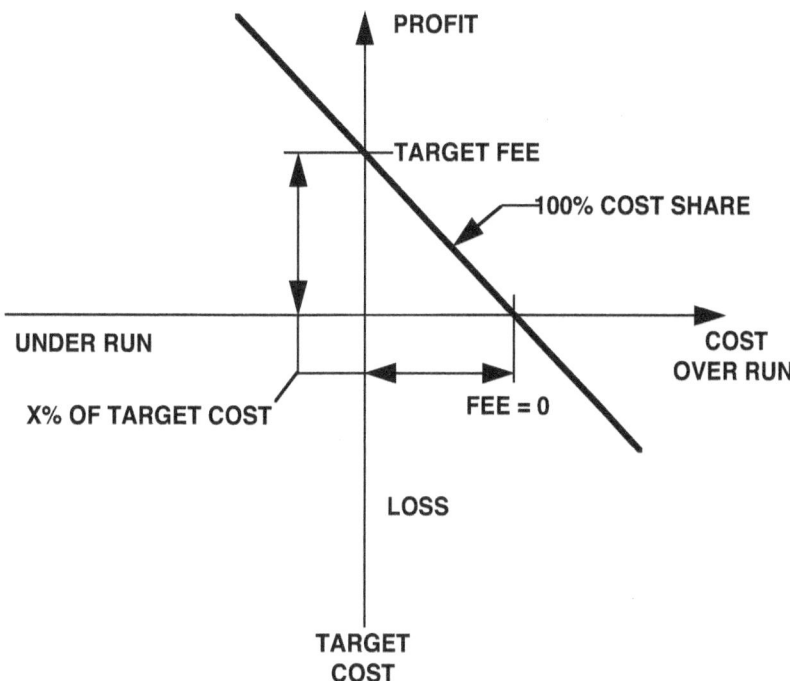

Figure 12-1 Fixed Price Cost-Fee Relationship

B. Cost Plus Percent of Cost (CPPC)

At the other end of the spectrum is a contract for services on a time and materials basis. Here, the buyer takes all the risk and is exposed to whatever the cost turns out to be. To at least assure that those costs are real, the smart buyer must have access to the seller's data on cost of labor, the hours expended, and proof

of the cost of the materials. The seller must be willing to "open his books" to justify his costs. Under these
conditions, the contract must provide for that information and agreement on the percentage of cost that will be profit. Generally, commercial forms of this type of arrangement would be called cost plus a percent of cost. This contract form is sometimes used for construction or contracts for services as directed by the buyer. Because of the lack of definition, it is the poorest form of what is called a *cost reimbursable contract* in which the buyer is liable for the full amount of costs legitimately incurred in the conduct of the work.

In the case of a cost plus percent of cost contract, the seller is actually incentivized to increase cost because profit is a percentage of whatever the cost turns out to be. The buyer's only recourse is to stop the job.   The only possible up side to the buyer in a cost plus percent of cost contract is that the buyer can direct changes at will without renegotiating the contract. But not having a paper trail of changes generally leads to disagreements when the bill is presented. Because of this and the reverse incentive on cost, most government entities do not permit cost plus percent of cost contracts to be used in their procurements. You shouldn't either!

Risk and its Implications to Contracts
In the commercial product market place, the development cost of the product is usually borne by the seller, who retains the ownership rights of the product design to sell into the larger market place. On the other hand, there are cases when the buyer seeks the development of a product and wishes to own the rights to the design at the completion of development, even if the buyer intends to continue buying from the same seller. An example might be that the buyer wishes to have multiple sources of supply, or sees the product as a vital part of the buy-

er's product line. In this case the buyer may pay the seller to do the development.

In contracting with the US Government for major facilities or defense systems, there is no commercial market, and in most cases the government does not want the resulting product sold to any other buyers such as foreign countries. This is called a monopsony. In these cases, the government usually insists on all rights of ownership and therefore pays for the development of the design and production tooling in many cases, reserving the right to put other sellers in business, if necessary to have multiple sources of supply.

A. Development risk

If you make a deal to develop a product or system for a customer application or use, even if it is similar to something you have done before, it involves some risk. First, there is the risk that it will take more effort to complete the development work than you think. Second, you don't know exactly what the product will consist of until you have finished the design, and therefore what it will in fact cost. It is therefore very unwise, even foolhardy, to bid a fixed production price before you have done the development work. It is also unwise to bid the development fixed price unless you are prepared to make a substantial additional internal investment in the outcome. Generally, we would not wish to do that if the customer paying for the development will own the design after it is developed.

The Rolls Royce L1011 story

In the late 1960s, Lockheed and McDonnell Douglas and the major engine suppliers were locked in a vicious competition for share in the wide-body passenger aircraft market. Rolls-Royce contracted with Lockheed to deliver a specified number of

RB211 Fan-jet engines for the new wide body Tri-Star L1011 aircraft at a fixed price. Aircraft engines are tailored for and uniquely integrated into the designs of specific aircraft, and both designs depend on each other. This engine promised to be a very quiet and fuel-efficient unit compared to any other engine then in existence, but much development work remained to be done. Rolls was happy because the development launched a new family of engines, derivatives of which could be sold for many other aircraft. Lockheed was happy because it was getting a superior engine at a fixed price that would competitively position the air-craft without risk of added development costs. [8]

Rolls Royce encountered serious problems during development of the RB211. None of these were show stopping, but the costs incurred pushed the prestigious Rolls Royce into bankruptcy and nearly took Lockheed with it. Lockheed which thought it had a bullet proof arrangement with Rolls, found itself without engines, a situation that turned customers to the competitor DC-10. The British government rescued Rolls Royce, but Rolls never fully re-covered.   Lockheed was forced by its banks to get loan guarantees for its loans backing its own development costs. Did Lockheed get what it thought it would for a fixed price? It did not. The contract was renegotiated to a new schedule and cost. Eventually the engines and the aircraft proved to be a technically superior combination.   But the L1011 program never broke even.

B. Multi year economic risks

Contracts that span more than two years involve a significant risk associated with economic factors. As an example, in the early1970's the US annual inflation rate exceeded 12% at times, fueled in part by the Arab oil embargo, and the so-called stagfla-

---

[8] Beyond the Horizons – The Lockheed Story
Walter J. Boyne   St. Martins Press 1998 p 357

tion of the Carter years. The annual cost of money in those times rose to 17 %. A seller with a fixed price contract signed in the early 70's with completion late in the decade would have been forced to absorb cost increases of 20% or more. It was even worse if one had to borrow.

C. Dealing with Government

As mentioned earlier, governments, whether local, state, or federal, create monopsonies for many of the products they buy. If you are a construction contractor for public works projects, or if you are a defense contractor bidding work from the federal government, there is effectively only one customer. The risk in this is that the buyer may unilaterally establish terms of contracting with no free market check and balance to mitigate this unilateral power. Under these circumstances, the buying agency often chooses a contracting form with terms that do not fit the real objectives of the procurement. The only game in town can be a bad game indeed. Many defense contracts have been agreed to that were totally inappropriate for either party because bidders were not willing to say "no thanks" to a big but bad opportunity; The U.S. Navy's ill-fated A-12 program was a classic example.[9] In the end it did no justice to the buyer or seller.

Many government entities have the experience and the integrity to have standard contracting terms that are equitable and sensible. The federal government, for example, has the Federal Acquisition Regulations (FARs), which originated in the Department of Defense. They also have provisions for tailoring these terms to the unique needs of the specific procurement. So again

---

[9] *A Plane That Never Was Could Still Cost Us a Bundle* Philip Dine St. Louis Post Dispatch March 8, 1998

the right approach is frank discussion before the bidding process begins to seek to modify the terms that are problematic.

D. Let the seller *and* buyer beware

Even if competitors will do so, integral managers on the seller's side will not play the only game in town. They will seek to convince the buyer of the potential dangers of the terms of his game, and if they cannot do so, they will walk away from a bad bid. Their responsibility to their stakeholders demands it. If the buyers are worth a hoot, they will listen to the potential supplier who will refuse to bid on the seller's terms, and will have more respect for that potential bidder. If the buyers will not listen, they are not worth making a contract with in any case. The buyers, by the same token should beware of a seller who will accept any terms without question.

Effective Cost Reimbursable Contracts

A. Cost Plus Fixed Fee (CPFF)

Cost plus fixed fee contracts are usually used when the buyer and seller are not certain about what is to be bought or the problems that might be encountered. To reduce the incentive for the seller to spend more time on the job than necessary, sometimes the fee is defined as a percent of the estimated or target cost, and does not change in dollar amount even if the cost exceeds the estimate (which it usually will). This type of contract, which also requires full disclosure of cost basis to the buyer, is called *Cost plus Fixed Fee*, and is used when neither buyer nor seller knows what problems may arise that change the direction and cost of the effort.

B. Specifying what you want to buy

CPFF contracts are not desirable if buyers know exactly what they want to buy. On the other hand, fixed price contracts are inappropriate unless what is being purchased has no uncertainties at all. If uncertainties do exist, fixed price contracts really are not fixed at all. If the buyers are going to own the rights to all data that comes out of a development effort, they should pay the seller's costs to do that job, so a cost reimbursable contract form is most appropriate. It is wise to create a contract that clearly delineates the requirements and objectives of the buyer for what is to be furnished. In doing so, a contract form is appropriate that incentivizes the seller to do what is necessary to exceed those requirements and meet the objectives. Properly done, the incentives dramatically affect the profit the seller can make depending on how well the requirements and objectives are met. These must be objectively defined and measurable. The following section describes some of those forms of contract.

More Complex Contract Forms Tailored to the Task and Risks to both Parties

A. Simple Form of Cost Plus Incentive Fee (CPIF)

Figure 12-2 shows an example of how a simple cost plus incentive fee contract works, where only cost is incentivized.

The principle here is that while seller's costs are covered, profit ought to be a function of performance: An excellent job should yield an excellent profit; an average job should result in an average profit; A poor job should result in no profit. What is excellent and what is poor must be well defined. At target cost and target performance, (expected or average contract performance) the target fee, which is a percent of target cost, is earned. Since the contract is cost reimbursable, the buyer still has the liability for all cost once the minimum fee position has been reached.

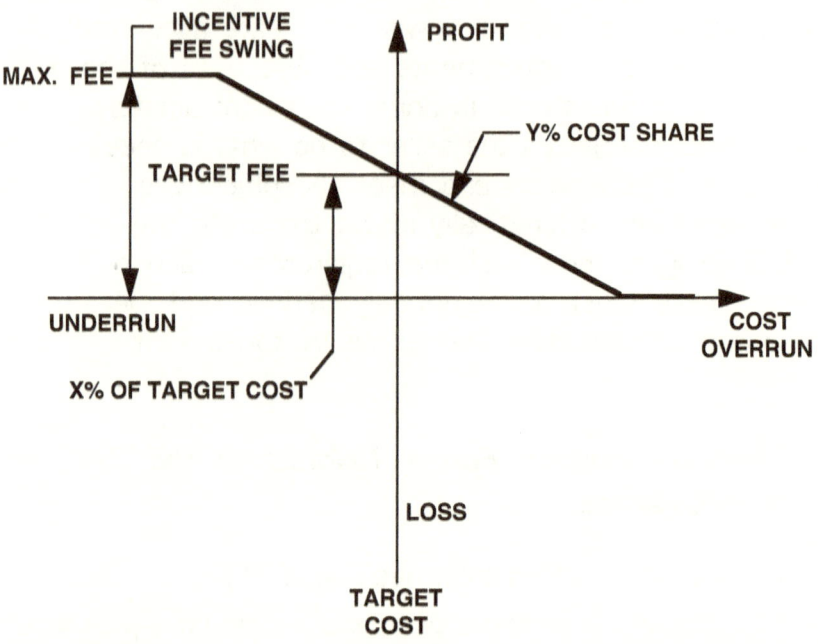

Figure 12-2 A Simple CPIF Cost Profit Relationship

B. Compound or Multiple Performance Incentives

The use of a CPIF form of contract with cost only incentives is a waste of a good tool. Multiple incentives provide the seller with guidance on the strategy for buyer satisfaction

In figure 12-3 we see an example of how a multiple incentive plan CPIF contract might work for the hybrid car example discussed earlier in this book.

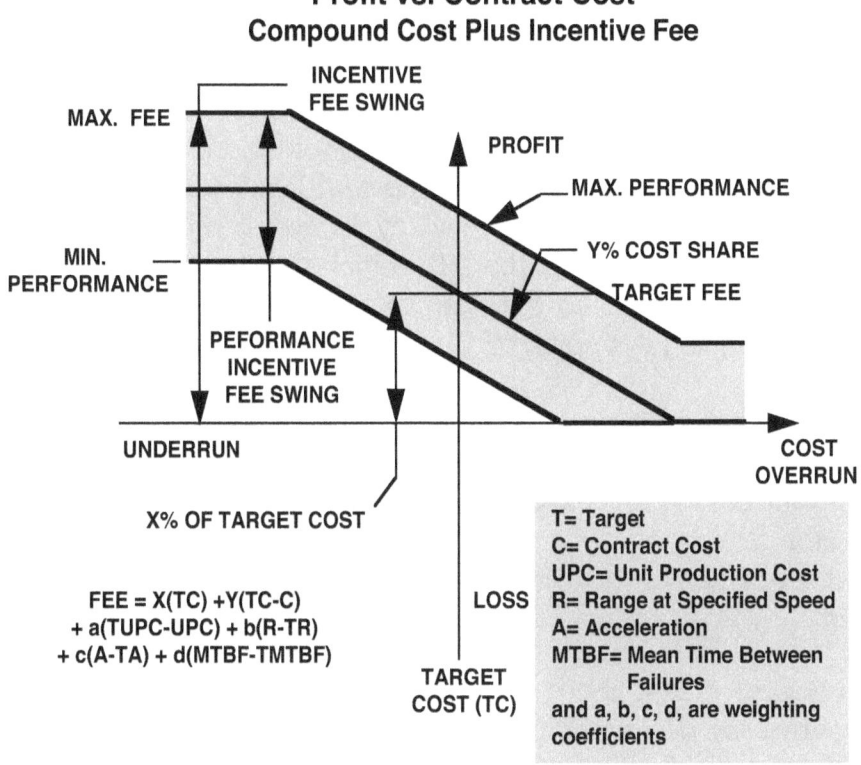

Profit vs. Contract Cost
Compound Cost Plus Incentive Fee

$$FEE = X(TC) + Y(TC-C) + a(TUPC-UPC) + b(R-TR) + c(A-TA) + d(MTBF-TMTBF)$$

T= Target
C= Contract Cost
UPC= Unit Production Cost
R= Range at Specified Speed
A= Acceleration
MTBF= Mean Time Between Failures
and a, b, c, d, are weighting coefficients

Figure 12-3 Multiple Incentive CPIF
Cost Profit Relationship For a Hybrid Auto Development

Let's assume that the buyer is a state highway agency that wants to develop a viable hybrid auto for production that meets certain criteria. If the vehicle meets these criteria, the state will invest in the roadway and power utilities to implement the system.

The key performance parameters are battery powered range at a specified speed, acceleration capability on batteries, average unit production cost of a pre-production sample of 50 vehicles, with a specified mean time between failures and an economical maintenance plan. Development cost is also important, but within limits, the buyer is willing to trade additional development cost to achieve a lower unit production cost and better vehicle performance. Schedule is only important insofar as it affects the state's next long range planning cycle, which will occur in four years. The state wants the 50 vehicles delivered three years from contract award so they can be tested for a year before the budget planning cycle starts.

We now have six or seven performance parameters that can be used to tell the contractor what it takes to maximize profit. Contract cost in this example is development cost plus the cost of pilot production. Unit Production Cost is the pilot production cost less any non-recurring cost divided by the 50 units delivered.

Development cost should be a fairly small fraction of the total incentive fee pool if the buyer wants the other performance objectives to be pursued. Performance in meeting or exceeding the requirements and achieving the objectives should form the majority of an incentive fee.

The state agency must decide on some value statements about each of these performance parameters, both individually and relative to each other. It must also decide the minimum acceptable outcomes for each parameter, the target values, and also the maximum objective it will pay to achieve.

The target values may or may not be halfway between the minimum acceptable and the maximum desired values. What they actually should be is the expected outcome for target development cost. In principle, an equitable contract would result in the developer in the aggregate having as much opportunity to make maximum profit as to make none. In this case there is no advantage to the buyer to complete the contract deliveries early, but there is a strong disadvantage for being late, so the schedule incentive is penalty only.

The beauty of this contract form when properly definitized is that it forces both buyer and seller to think about the strategy to best achieve the desired outcome. It results in a real meeting of the minds.

Once the contract is signed, the buyer must step back and let the seller do the job and try to maximize profit, guided by the incentive plan. Any direction by the buyers makes them liable for a constructive contract change. The seller must provide continuing visibility of accomplishment to the buyer and demonstrate compliance with the contract. Performance against the incentives must be measured objectively and dispassionately in accordance with the methods outlined in the contract. This approach instills a discipline on both buyer and seller from start to finish, that is very beneficial in almost all cases.

C. Cost Plus Award Fee (CPAF)

I have never been a fan of this contracting form, because it is very subjective, and encourages meddling and gaming by the buyer. Its proponents say that there are some things that cannot be measured by a dollar value such as human life in manned space programs; or, that what is important may change from one period to the next. What it really does is to remove all effective decision power from the seller, and makes the seller try to please the buyer to the maximum extent possible. If the buyer is capricious, and some are, the project can lose all coherence. There is no balance of power in this arrangement.

D. Fixed Price Incentive (FPI)

Figure 12-4 shows the cost/profit relationship for this FPI contract form. It is really a cross between a cost plus incentive fee and a firm fixed price contract. It differs from a CPIF form in that it has a point of total cost assumption by the seller. That is, at some cost above target, the cost share borne by the seller goes to 100%, and the buyer has no additional cost liability. Below that cost, multiple incentives can be employed similar to the compound CPIF example. But generally, cost share by the seller is much higher than in a CPIF contract.

Profit vs. Contract Cost
Fixed Price Incentive

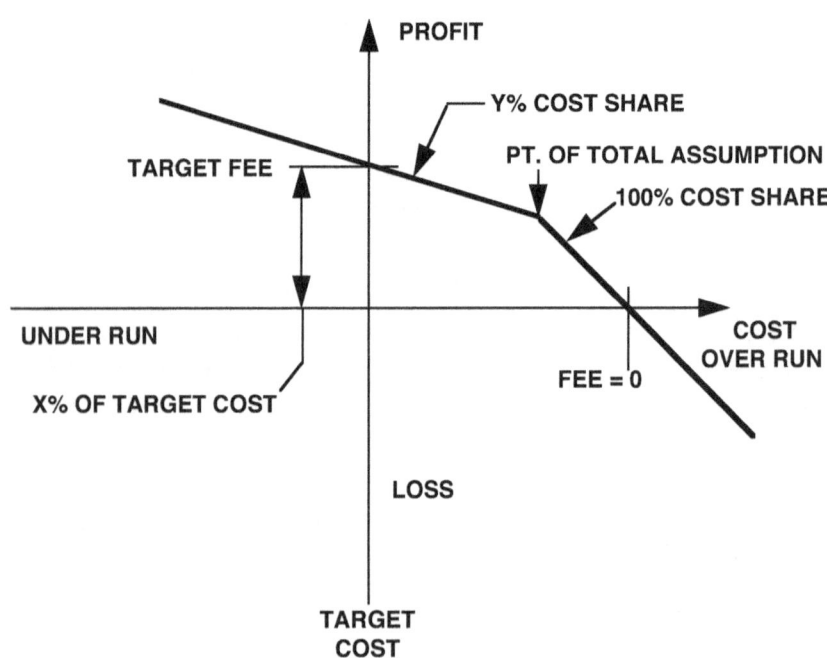

Figure 12-4 Fixed Price Incentive Contract
Cost Fee Relationship

This contract form makes sense when the product is well defined, but has some cost uncertainty and performance above some minimum threshold is desirable.

It must be recognized that if the seller's cost gets close to the point of total assumption, the seller should and will act as though the contract were FFP

E. Cost plus Incentive Fee with a Ceiling

A CPIF contract with a ceiling is a hybrid wherein if the cost exceeds some value above target, the contractor assumes all additional cost just as in an FPI contract. Generally, neither party expected to be there, and it is usually the result of a renegotiated CPIF contract that has run into major difficulty.

12.4 Important Tests for Choosing the Right Contract Form

We can summarize some simple tests for the applicability of any contract form. They are applicable whether you are a buyer or seller.

A. If you know exactly what you want and can buy it out of a catalog, a fixed price purchase agreement will be fine provided you have a way to verify that you got what you paid for.

B. A product isn't off the shelf if it isn't in stock or currently in production. The restart of an old production line creates risks in process replication, and requires proof that the production yields the same product. In short, this situation is not a good candidate for a fixed-price contract—from the buyer's or seller's perspective.

C. If development is required, the seller should not offer it for a fixed price if the buyer is going to have ownership of the design. There is no such thing as fixed price development. Someone is going to have to pay the piper in the event of unforeseen problems. The seller would be justified in covering any development overrun if retaining rights to the product design would allow the seller to recoup those losses in other markets. Even then, the seller should make sure that his or her bosses know that they may have to pony up additional funds to complete the job. Doing it for customer good will is generally unwise because good will has a way of dissipating as in "What have you done for me lately?"

D. A buyer who buys fixed price and makes even the smallest change will pay dearly for the change, which will have a high profit margin because of the seller's risk. So a fixed price contract won't limit a buyer's liability unless the requirements stay fixed. Even then there is no guarantee. (See the L1011 example)

E. A Cost plus incentive fee contract offers by far the highest integrity method of contracting for anything that requires significant development effort in which the buyer will have primary rights.

F. If neither buyer or seller knows what is needed without substantial design iteration, a CPFF contract makes the most sense, but it should be conducted with the discipline of a CPIF contract to the maximum extent possible, with a written trail for all changes. Buyers often abuse this type of contract, and the seller often lets them. One good approach is to start with the more fluid CPFF contract and then convert it to a more rigorous form when the uncertainties have been resolved.

G. Never use a cost plus percent of cost contract for anything.

12.5 The Dangers of Non-linearities in Cost-Fee Relationships

A few observations on non-linearities in incentivized contracts are worthwhile before leaving the subject of contract forms. Non-linearities such as the break point at the point of total assumption in an FPI contract, or dead bands around cost targets, cost-share ratio changes, or other performance parameter functions, have their place in tailoring a contracting plan. But they can result in undesired behavior depending on where the buyer and seller find themselves later in time. If you choose to use such elegant finery, be sure to conduct simulations and role playing to avoid counterproductive incentives.

12.6 What if the Contract Becomes Inoperable?

Contracts are not chiseled in stone. There are times when the best laid plans and contracts encounter a problem where the contract tells the seller to do something that has been overtaken by events, which if continued would be counterproductive. This happens. Remember the pre-amble to the contract I mentioned earlier? Don't ever be afraid to propose changing a contract that for some reason has become dysfunctional in the context of current events.

12.7 Your Signature is Your Bond

NEVER SIGN ANYTHING YOU HAVEN'T READ AND <u>UNDERSTOOD</u>

This is as important in your private life a s in your professional life. I had a boss who once told me, "You can sign for me on any document or commitment until you screw up. If you do, you will no longer even be allowed to sign your own name." A true vote of confidence, but with a sobering admonition. I got the point.

Your signature means something. In a high integrity environment it means everything. It says you have made a commitment about the validity of what you signed. Whether you're signing a con-tract, a requirements specification, a personal loan or an insurance policy, read all of the fine print. Someone put it there for a reason. If you are authoring or approving a document, and you or someone else cannot understand what it says, it probably isn't a good document.

Chapter 13 Motivations

13.0 Introduction

Early in this book I asserted that the most important asset of an Enterprise or project is its people and their motivation. This is particularly true of the largest segment of the work force that creates and builds the products of the Enterprise. We talked about the job of the integral manager in balancing the needs of all stakeholders. We discussed some of the incentives that are used to motivate the senior managers in an Enterprise to meet the objectives of the share-holders, and the implications of these diverse and seemingly conflicting forces. But how about lower and middle management and other employees? How do incentives at various levels of the Enterprise motivate desired behavior?

13.1 Financial Incentives as a Motivation for the Workforce

Unless you are at the highest level of management -- where by the SEC definition you are "an insider", the price of a share of stock is almost entirely beyond your control. We used to think that earnings per share drive share price, but so do many other factors. Recently, the perception of future stock appreciation, sometimes based on pure speculation has driven technology stocks even in the absence of earnings. What you and everyone who reports to you can affect directly is profit of your part of the Enterprise. Saving cost increases profitability, and profit after tax is earnings. Managers and employees sometimes make decisions about use of company or customer resources in their care that don't support the goals of the Enterprise. It has always seemed to me that the proper way to operate my portion of an Enterprise was to consider the Enterprise resources that I was entrusted to manage as if they were acquired by my sweat equity. Spending them wisely was as important as spending my own hard-earned money. I have been surprised and disappointed to see that some managers don't share that philosophy.

It is top management's job to establish the proper motivations for everyone in the Enterprise to work toward, and here is where they often screw it up. Accountability for commitments made in response to these motivations is an important part of this problem.

What motivates the first line manager in today's environment? And what effective motivations are available to the work force? One element is clearly being appreciated as an important member of the team with an opportunity to grow to higher levels of responsibility and compensation in the organization. Twenty to thirty years ago, participative management, management by objectives, and collaborative management teams were popular concepts to motivate lower levels of management in this context, but for some reason they have lost their luster since then. Stock options are the most popular incentives today, particularly in start-up companies. Today with mergers and buyouts, first line and middle management have far less confidence about their long-term prospects with any company, and this has a chilling effect on both enthusiasm for the Enterprise objectives and the trust for higher levels. If this is to change, a major change in today's short-sighted philosophy of management will have to take place. The employees will have to be treated as a valued resource instead of an annoying expense.

I am convinced by experience that people want to succeed and have high self-worth,[10] and will work beyond your fondest expectations if they understand the goal, feel valued, and are

---

[10] *The Human Side of Enterprise*   Douglas MacGregor; McGraw Hill 1960
   The Professional Manager, Douglas MacGregor; McGraw Hill 1968

treated fairly. I recall an occasion, while in one of our manufacturing shops, I was introduced to a long-time lead technician who was also a union shop steward. He described a problem that had been going on for some time with an electronics package design that required re-work of every unit. He proposed a solution that, if successful, would simplify the design, and also would eliminate his job. Because of his seniority, he wasn't worried about losing his job, but I was struck by his sincere desire to fix a problem that was costing us money unnecessarily. He had thought about that problem and tried to get the design modified, but the engineers were "too busy" with other problems to fix it.

As a result of that discussion, some priorities were reordered. This individual was not unique among long term shop employees or employees in general. Most of us like to be part of a winning team with the pride of accomplishments we make. A key part of feeling valued is getting sincere recognition for our contribution.

Many organizations have programs that recognize outstanding work or ideas with cash awards or plaques. These are fine, but can become distorted or diluted by over use, misuse, and game playing. Employees can usually participate to some extent in a company's stock performance through their tax-deferred retirement savings accounts like employee stock ownership plans (ESOP), IRAs or 401k plans. But that typically is a future benefit and far removed from their day to day performance.

An effective approach to team building in my view is some form of profit- sharing by every non-management employee having more than say, three years of seniority.

13.2 Sharing the benefits of success.

Where is it written that only management is smart enough to make the right decisions in an Enterprise? I have seen ample evidence that today's work force is knowledgeable to an extent never seen before. Employees are capable of participating in the operation of the Enterprise and making improvements in their part of the operation when management doesn't even recognize a deficiency exists. Why not enlist their help and let them share in the rewards of the improvements that result, remembering that we said the job of management included coaching.

One implementation might be to establish a profit target for the measurable business unit that represents a normal expected result. If that target were exceeded for the year, 20 % of that additional profit would go to a fund that would be divided among all non-management employees within the business unit.

As an example, consider a business unit with annual sales of $1.5 billion and 6,000 employees, 5500 of which are eligible for the program. Assume a target profit of 10% and a realized profit of 15%.   20% of the difference of $75 Million would be $15M represents an average of about $2,700 in profit sharing per eligible employee.

Aside from the direct tie to performance, two other benefits would accrue. First is involvement. When you share the rewards, you also share the responsibilities. Second, it might mitigate the often heard complaint that the company is making a big profit and rewarding the management at the expense of the work force.

13.3 Conclusion

The following table, a reprise from Chapter 1 serves to remind us what engenders effective team performance. If you want employees to exhibit the first four elements of integrity, you must Foster an environment that provides the last four elements.

WHAT'S IMPORTANT	ISSUE
• PROGRAM SUCCESS	• FIRST AND FORMOST
• PERFORMANCE	• RESULTS AND MEANS COUNT • ITS ABOUT PEOPLE
• INTEGRITY	• INITIATIVE • PLANNING • COMMITMENT • OWNERSHIP • COMMUNICATION • HONESTY • TEAMWORK • RECOGNITION

Table 13-1 Elements of Project Integrity

Those are the motivators for good work and a good work environment. Being a member of the team includes sharing in the financial stake of that team's performance.

Profit sharing seems a good way to financially back up the phrase "valued employee."

Chapter 14 Management Expectations

14.0 Putting It All Together

This final chapter offers an example of communicating the expectations of leadership to all levels.

14.1 Setting and communicating expectations for management

Motivation to manage in the way desired requires communication of expectations. In the Enterprise that I managed, as our environment went through some dramatic changes we found that we needed to update and state our expectations of each other, and our subordinates. A large part of this book is the result of three papers that I wrote to express my expectations of how we needed to manage and operate in this changing environment, building on the lessons of those who preceded me. While a framework based on our past experience existed, significant changes had occurred -- not only in the legal and business environment, but in at least two generations of management and supervision.

Some of our current management and administrative team suggested that we should develop a new statement of leadership expectations as a handbook given to all new members of supervision, and as reminders for all existing members of supervision and management from top to bottom. What follows is excerpted from the result of their work.

14.2 An Example of Integral Management Expectations

This document captures the general expectations of all levels of management in the kind of environment that I support. it is mainly the work of a multi-level group of leaders from across our Enterprise. I have edited it to omit specific administrative processes and organization references not relevant to this discussion. It brings together the many threads that when woven together define the fabric of the mantle of leadership. As such, it seemed a fitting conclusion to the book.

****

LEADERSHIP EXPECTATIONS

1.0 Preface:

The purpose of this document is to describe what is expected of a leader in our Enterprise. It applies to any job that requires the exercise of leadership --coded supervisor, group engineer, manager, director, project leader, assistant program manager, project engineer, executive, and product development team leader.

What follows is more a "guide" supporting a philosophy than a "how-to manual". However, there *are* actions described herein that every leader *must* take. Most importantly, this document describes what we expect of each other as leaders in this Enterprise and will be the basis against which we will evaluate all levels of leadership.

2.0 Management Philosophy

This organization's management philosophy has been forged by almost 40 years of success and the experiences accumulated during six generations of management, programs, mistakes, and triumphs. We state it here to remind ourselves that these tenets describe what we expect of each other in the conduct of our work.

2.1 People -- Our Important Asset

An Enterprise is only as good as its people make it. How well they apply their talents and energy to our programs and business objectives determines whether we succeed or not. They either make success happen or prevent it from happening. Leadership must create a framework of trust and an environment that offers the opportunity for all our employees to contribute to the full extent of their abilities, with growth limited only by their initiative, and be rewarded and promoted on the basis of their performance and value to the organization. Our leaders must set high expectations for performance, communicate those expectations, empower their people, coach them to help them succeed, and evaluate their performance and achievements fairly.

2.2 Program Success Is Our Success

We believe that our decisions should be driven by the long-term benefits to the programs we are working on, not the immediate benefits to our Enterprise. The long-term satisfaction of our customers and our contracts is the key to our success. We will *not* make choices based on short term gains at the expense of that long-term outcome. Simply put, what is right for the program will be right for our Enterprise in the long run.

2.3 Performance Measured by Results and How They are Achieved

Results are the primary measure of performance, but the means by which those results are achieved are also important.

2.4 Integrity is the Most Important of This Organization's Expectations

Our relationships with our customers, with our suppliers, and with each other cannot be successful without trust, and trust requires integrity at all levels at all times. Seven key ingredients of integrity apply to every one of us in our work. They are: **initia-**

tive, planning, commitment, ownership, communication, honesty, and **teamwork.** We expect these of everyone in a position of leadership! And not just when things are going well, but most importantly when things are going badly.

Initiative:
integrity includes the willingness to take the initiative when you see a problem or the need for action. People who take pride in their work don't wait to be told what to do; when they see a problem that needs fixing, they act accordingly.

Planning:
To do a credible job of any kind, one must plan. This means thinking about whom your customers are -- who depends on you to do your part of the job by a time and at a cost consistent with the need. In order to make a commitment and meet it, a credible plan that considers the "what ifs" of the task must exist. A serious commitment to a job requires willingness to do the planning, to determine what to measure against, and to provide the follow-up and decisions that lead to the fulfillment of that commitment.

Ownership
Having taken the initiative and done the planning to allow an achievable commitment to be made, integrity requires the leader, the group, and each individual to take ownership of that job and that commitment to see that it happens.

Communication:
Communication is a key element in motivation. When people know what is expected of them, and if they are listened to when

they contribute ideas, they are more apt to make a personal commitment and take ownership. We need to communicate our goals, strategies, objectives, and expectations. Countless studies show that productivity suffers where communication is poor. The more complex the work and the greater the number of organizational interfaces, the greater the need for effective flow of information, both formal and informal, upward and downward as well as laterally. Honest communications engender mutual trust and respect.

Honesty:

Actions speak many times louder than words. Communication must be honest to be effective, and the actions that follow the communication must be congruent with it. If there is to be trust between leaders and employees, team members, and customers, then honesty is required in all parts of the endeavor. That means, for example, being willing to admit mistakes, not hiding bad news, and examining and resolving conflicts in objectives in an open and productive way.

This requires creating an environment that encourages all of the foregoing and leads to and rewards teamwork.

Teamwork:

"We versus they" is not the language of a team. When people build bridges rather than walls around what they do, teamwork will be improved, and conflicts in objectives between functions will be minimized. If more of us would ask each other, "what are you trying to achieve? And how can I help you achieve your objectives while I achieve mine?" we could find more win-win solutions with productive results.

3.0 The Role of Leadership
3.1 Our Relationship to our Programs

Earlier we said that our success as an organization is; measured by the success of the programs we work on. This level of commitment is one of our great strengths, and we expect to apply it to all of our future programs. However, the days when we were exclusively dedicated to one customer are over and one program are over. Our Enterprise has come to take on a completely new character over the past few years. We are influenced by new, added business objectives and changes in defense funding. For the first time in our history, we find ourselves with many smaller programs competing for resources. We cannot expect our prior experience to provide all of the answers in this new environment. What we must do is find ways to apply the principles that served us so well in the single program environment -- particularly our sense of commitment -- to the situation we face today. As leaders, we will be the ones that make this happen.

The requirements of smaller programs coupled with the need for efficient use of resources has decreased the need for organization management and placed more focus on project oriented leadership. The Integrated Product Development Team (PDT) is a new name but not a new concept in our experience; what is new is that there are many more projects. PDT's do not replace our organizational structure; they coexist with that structure. We can all expect to have some contact with PDT's. We may not work with them directly, but we may be committing our organization and our people to them. Leaders are expected to support program needs as negotiated with the program, to provide employees assigned to PDT's with the authority to speak for the organization on that PDT, and to provide the commitment necessary to achieve program success.

3.2 Our Relationship to our Employees
As members of this Enterprise's leadership, we are *the* link in communication with our employees. Employees need and deserve to understand clearly the impact and consequences of

their involvement. It is essential that we understand our strategy, objectives, and policies -- and the reasons for them -- and are able to communicate them to our employees. Our employees can only commit to our objectives when they fully understand their own relationship to those objectives.

We are also expected to listen to our employees and provide a forum for upward communication, a "bottom-up" motivator. A synergistic relationship with our employees can be developed when we listen and invite them to participate in the decision making process. Management by Walking Around, staff meetings, brown bag lunches, skip level meetings, etc. are some effective techniques for communicating. We are all expected to use them.

As leaders, there are four skills we must persistently use and improve:
- Listening
- Soliciting and encouraging participation
- Providing feedback
- Empowering and coaching those who report to us.

Some might protest that "I don't have the time". *We cannot afford not to have the time!* Listening to the people we lead is an ability each of us is expected to have, and to continuously improve. Equally important, our everyday actions will be important in determining the willingness of those around us to communicate. Make an effort to know each employee; effective and frank communication begins with mutual trust and respect. There will be occasions when you don't agree with what you hear. Don't hide your point of view, but honestly present the facts and all points of view to the employees.

3.3 Empowerment and Coaching

Empowering our employees means providing them the latitude and authority to perform the *whole job.* But the really difficult and crucial part is clearly defining the job and providing guidance, expectations, goals, feedback and encouragement.

A key to the concept of empowerment can be found in the way we have tried to describe program requirements in the past. In this parallel, we specify the "targets" we wish to achieve. We also specify a higher goal toward which we are encouraged to strive. Finally, we specify what we consider to be the minimum acceptable performance. We often have reward systems (called incentives) that tie the minimums, targets, and goals to our business success. Within that framework we have the ability (the freedom) to do our job over the several years of design, trades, test, and production in order to deliver within those parameters.

We need to apply that way of thinking to the empowerment of our work force. To do this takes some really hard work and thought about what we want our employees to accomplish in any project, task or assignment. It requires that those of us in positions of leadership think in the following terms:

    - Determine and articulate the end goals: what is important and what is not. Also communicate the targets and what is the minimum acceptable outcome (e.g., technical performance, cost, schedule).

    - Assure that rewards (and Performance Appraisals) are tied to goals and requirements.

    - Clearly describe the extent of the decision-making authority. Which decisions can be made independently? Which can be independently, but with prompt notification? Which cannot be made without higher approval or consultation? Remember, the old adage "Everyone has a boss" still applies.

- Describe how you, as the leader, expect to be kept informed.

- Be available and make clear that an important, positive characteristic of a good performer and an effective team is knowing when to ask for help.

- Don't take the job out of the hands of the employees with overbearing, detailed direction. Let the employees do the work; encourage, show confidence and provide support.

- *Always* achieve a common understanding of the commitments being made!

Our role in the empowerment of our employees should lead us to develop and emphasize the *coaching dimension* of managing. The fundamental concepts of coaching are perfectly suited to the team settings we must foster.

- Working together as a team to meet the organization's goals.

- Making sure everyone is contributing; conversely, doing something about those who are not contributing.

- Training the employees in the skills needed to accomplish the goals.

- Understanding every member of the team: what motivates each of them? What are their needs?

- Putting the team "on the playing field" and letting *them* perform.

- Being there! Being available, open, and a contributor when things aren't going well or according to plan.

A coach believes in and supports the people on the team, knowing that all members want to do their job, do their best, and contribute to the success of the team. If they don't, the coach has missed something very important and must take corrective action. The coach plays a huge role in the mental attitude of the team members.

3.4 Upward Evaluation
Upward evaluation *is* communication. Every member of our leadership is expected to participate in the upward evaluation process. The employees' perception of those in leadership positions affects morale and performance, and is a source of feedback and guidance to the leader being evaluated.

We have an established process available to everyone for upward evaluation. It is called "Upward Performance Feedback." That process protects the anonymity of the employees and provides help and guidance from the professionals in Human Resources. Our policy neither requires nor prohibits the sharing of results with the leader's manager. However, sharing the feedback you receive with your manager in a frank and constructive atmosphere will provide a basis for your own personal growth, a development plan, and additional feedback on performance.

The upward evaluation process will be a waste of time if its results are not objectively evaluated and translated into a plan of action for the leader's personal growth.

4.0 Performance: Expectations and Evaluation

4.1 Setting Expectations and Opportunities
Our goal for our employees is that each:
> - Knows what performance is expected.
> - Is given challenging assignments
> - Is assigned duties consistent with abilities, training, and aspirations
> - Has access to personal development planning and opportunities.

Leaders should assess their organizations against these goals and establish corrective steps where deficiencies exist. Every employee must be able to address these goals with a person in leadership.

The remainder of this chapter deals with important details in how we evaluate and reward. They will be of no use to the reader unless the goals just stated are understood and taken on as *personal* goals.

4.2 Performance Evaluation

Our pay policy stresses two fundamental principles regarding employee compensation:
  - *Fairness:* To reward employees fairly for their relative contribution.
  - *Competitiveness:* To establish salaries that are competitive with pay rates at companies with whom we compete for business and personnel

To meet these objectives, Performance Appraisals (SPA), Ranking, and Pay for Performance must be considered together in a process that is one of our most important leader-ship functions.

4.3 The Performance Appraisal (SPA)
Performed properly, the SPA provides meaningful feed-back to the employees, establishes ranking, and also serves as a vehicle for personal development. The SPA must be *job relevant* and *credible* to the employee who will be rated. To be relevant, it should state what is necessary and only measure behavior and activities which are directly related to job performance. Unless the employee regards the factors being measured as valid and fair, the SPA will fail the test of credibility. The employee should understand the relative weighting of each of the factors, the ra-

tionale for each of the weights, and which are considered to be the most significant.

The two essential elements to relevance and credibility are the joint development of projected task descriptions and measurable performance standards. These standards must be pre-determined, objective, and clearly stated. The individual must be evaluated only on performance and not on factors beyond his or her control. Without careful attention to these factors, the SPA loses its meaning for both the good performers and those whose performance needs improvement.

Regularly scheduled and informal feedback sessions should be conducted once per quarter at a minimum. These reviews should be treated as confidential discussions between the employee and the reviewer. This frequent feedback will preclude surprises and allow for updates in cases where a task description has changed.

The SPA and the periodic reviews of task descriptions and accomplishments are among the most effective means of communication through which mutual trust and understanding are promoted. It is always more pleasurable to evaluate a good performer; however, as leaders, it is even more important to use the SPA and frequent reviews as an opportunity to counsel and improve the lesser performer. Given the new program and leadership relationships, and frequent use of product development teams, it is more important than ever that we do *joint appraisals* for employees who are located with the program to which they are assigned (and not their "home" organization). A fair evaluation of their performance must be influenced by the people supported with their work.

Joint appraisals are **mandatory** for these employees, and their "home supervisor" is expected to obtain and include the cognizant program leader's evaluation for each person. The contributors to the appraisal should participate in the interview(s) with the employee, jointly or separately. Joint evaluation shall be verified by both the supervisor's and program leader's signature on the evaluation.

In summary, SPA and periodic reviews should be *relevant* and *credible*. As leaders we need to:
- Identify projected annual tasks/ descriptions
- Develop measurable performance standards
- Conduct periodic reviews
- Perform an objective and reliable annual SPA
- Reach joint agreement/ obligation on means to enhance performance

4.4 Employee Ranking In compliance with our personnel policy, every salaried employee is ranked. This is an indispensable administrative function since it is the basis for merit and career decisions.

Our effectiveness in how we pay our people is a huge factor in our competitiveness. *How much* we pay sets our cost competitiveness; *who* we pay affects the ability to reward and retain the people most important to our success; *how fairly* we determine pay affects the morale of the entire organization.

We use an *objective* process for determining the proper pay level of each of its employees. That process will consider the relative value of each employee to the organization, the employee's compensation in comparison to ranking and the difficulty of the task assigned to the employee.

5.0 Ethics

We depend on the actions of our people, and not on a set of policies and procedures or "the system," to assure the integrity and ethics of our company. The *individual* is accountable for actions taken.

It is unrealistic to expect a statement about ethical behavior in our business and company that will cover all circumstances. But there are a few basics we *must* understand, and if we live by these basics, an ethical outcome will be almost assured.

- We are open and honest in *all* our actions:
with each other, our customers, and our suppliers

- We meet our commitments.
This means we are honest and realistic in the commitments we make.

- The rewards and opportunities offered to our   employees are based on performance and how they are achieved.

-We treat every employee with respect and value the contribution each makes to the organization.

Our "*Managing Diversity/ Valuing Differences*" training provides a clear focus and awareness of diversity issues. As leaders, we are expected to conduct ourselves in accordance with those principles.

6.0   We comply with the law and with all of the company's business practice and ethics policies.

Appendix 1
Design to Cost
Program Management Memo

Program Management Memoranda

PMM NO.		SHEET
PC&A	.11.0	1 OF 4
		DATE: 4 FEB 1974

CLASSIFIED BY: Unclass (BA174 2-4-)

SUBJECT (Product Name) DESIGN-TO-COST PROGRAM

PURPOSE To initiate the subject program and to establish organizational responsibilities. The Design to cost program will apply to the (Product Name)

REFERENCE (1) (Preliminary cost targets for Production Segment A @ unit 308 and Production Segment B @ unit 1000, to be issued).

BACKGROUND The Program will be incented to a target production cost consistent with Navy planning for an operational program, in a way similar to (a prior program) The selection of technology and the baseline designs to meet the (new product) performance objectives must also consider the effect on the unit production cost of those decisions and the subsequent design that evolves.

The estimated and actual performance in production will be continuously measured against the "Design to Cost" targets. It is incumbent upon MSD to set up the machinery necessary to establish and maintain target cost allocations for each major missile segment, together with the feedback and control necessary to influence the design toward an outcome consistent with those target costs. This PMM directs the creation of that machinery.

REQUIREMENTS The Design-To-Cost Program requires four basic ingredients to make it work:

1. Cost Target Allocation

   An allocation method which allocates targets by major missile and RB segment by branch, e.g., Manufacturing, Materiel, and Product Assurance. This allocation will be initially developed by the Program Office with assistance from Finance and the branches.

2. Review and Estimation of Cost

   The interaction between Engineering, Materiel, Manufacturing, Product Assurance and Finance needed to understand the labor and non-labor resources required to implement engineering design solutions,

81-	82- R. L. Paulick	83- F. B. McQuinny	ORIGINATOR J. F. Aterhold	ORGN 8074	DATE
84-	85- A E Simmons Fr 85-01 16 Oct 73	86-	APPROVED		
87- Smiley	88- O. E. Liggett	80- 2-7-74	PROGRAM MANAGER		

Program Management Memoranda

PMM NO.		SHEET
PC&A 11.0		2 of 4

SUBJECT
REQMTS: Cont'd.

(Product Name) DESIGN-TO-COST PROGRAM

2. Review and Estimation of Cost (Cont'd)

    with the necessary feedback to allow comparison of the estimated cost of a design with the target.

3. Compatible Cost Accumulation Structure

    A cost account structure which will allow the accumulation of actual costs at the segment level for the purpose of comparing those costs against the planned target costs.

4. Branch Commitments

    Commitment to resource estimates entered into a cost accumulation structure where it can be compared with targets; a resource plan for work under contract consistant with these resource estimates; corrective action when estimated or actual costs exceed target costs.

ACTION

Figure 1 gives the intent of the design-to-cost process and the general Roles of the various organizations.

Program Office

o   Provide the program management direction required to insure that the Design-to-Cost Program is implemented and sustained.

o   Establish major control-segment definition.

o   Initially allocate cost targets by major missile and RB segment, with help as required from Finance and the branches.

o   Approve the total target-cost plan, based on the target segment costs committed to by the branches. Maintain surveillance of the total plan, periodically review the design-to-cost status.

o   Review and approve procedures implementing the system.

Finance

o   In conjunction with each branch, identify each branch's cost-account structure for production, in accordance with the cost-target structure and the contract definition of repetitive production cost (RPC).

o   Devise and implement the controls, procedures, and cost-account structure to accumulate actual costs in appropriate categories.

Program
Management Memoranda

PMM NO.	SHEET
	3 OF 4
PO&A 11.0 (SUB-SECTION) DATE	
CLASSIFIED BY:	

SUBJECT (PRODUCT NAME)DESIGN-TO-COST PROGRAM

ACTION Cont'd.

Finance :   (Cont'd)

o   Translate the resource estimates and actuals provided by the performing branches into target and actual dollar costs by applying the appropriate rates and prorated shares of costs that cannot be charged directly against specific segments.

o   Provide periodic Financial status of the DTC program to   Program Office personnel and Enterprise Management.

Engineering :

The operation of the Design-to-Cost Program will involve the Producibility Team concept already in existence. As the design-responsibility for setting up and administering the procedures necessary to the design-to-cost process, consistent with this PMM and within the framework of existing disciplines to the maximum extent possible. This responsibility includes the following actions:

o   Establish and coordinate procedures for assessing and reporting current estimates of all branch resources required to produce the design.

o   Allocate target costs to lower levels of design and control.

o   Provide, for the current design standard characteristics model, periodic reports of design-to-cost status by control segment and branch to the   Program Office.

o   Notify the Program Office of any planned changes in allocation of target costs at major segment level.

o   Provide design information on a timely basis, to allow assessment of the cost of the design and to give feedback to the responsible design manager.

All branches that add cost to the product as delivered:

o   Establish procedures and suitable cost accounts to accumulate estimates and actuals of branch resources, with the necessary visibility for corrective action at the control segment level

Program Management Memoranda	PMM NO.	SHEET 4 OF 4
	SECTION: SUB-SECTION: DATE PC&A 11.0	
	CLASSIFIED BY:	

SUBJECT (PRODUCT NAME) DESIGN-TO-COST PROGRAM

ACTION Cont'd

All Branches Adding Cost to the Product as Delivered (cont.):

by the manager with functional design responsibility, or by the manager responsible for each procurement, fabrication, test, and logistics function contributing cost to the product.

o   Develop and commit to a resource estimate and enter the estimate into the cost accumulation structure where it will be compared to targets.

o   Develop and commit to a resource plan for work under contract which is consistent with the resource estimate. The committed to resources will be the plan entered into the Contract Budget System.

o   Take corrective design action when required to bring estimated or actual costs into line with the agreed-to-segment cost targets.

BUDGET This effort has no effect on current budget.

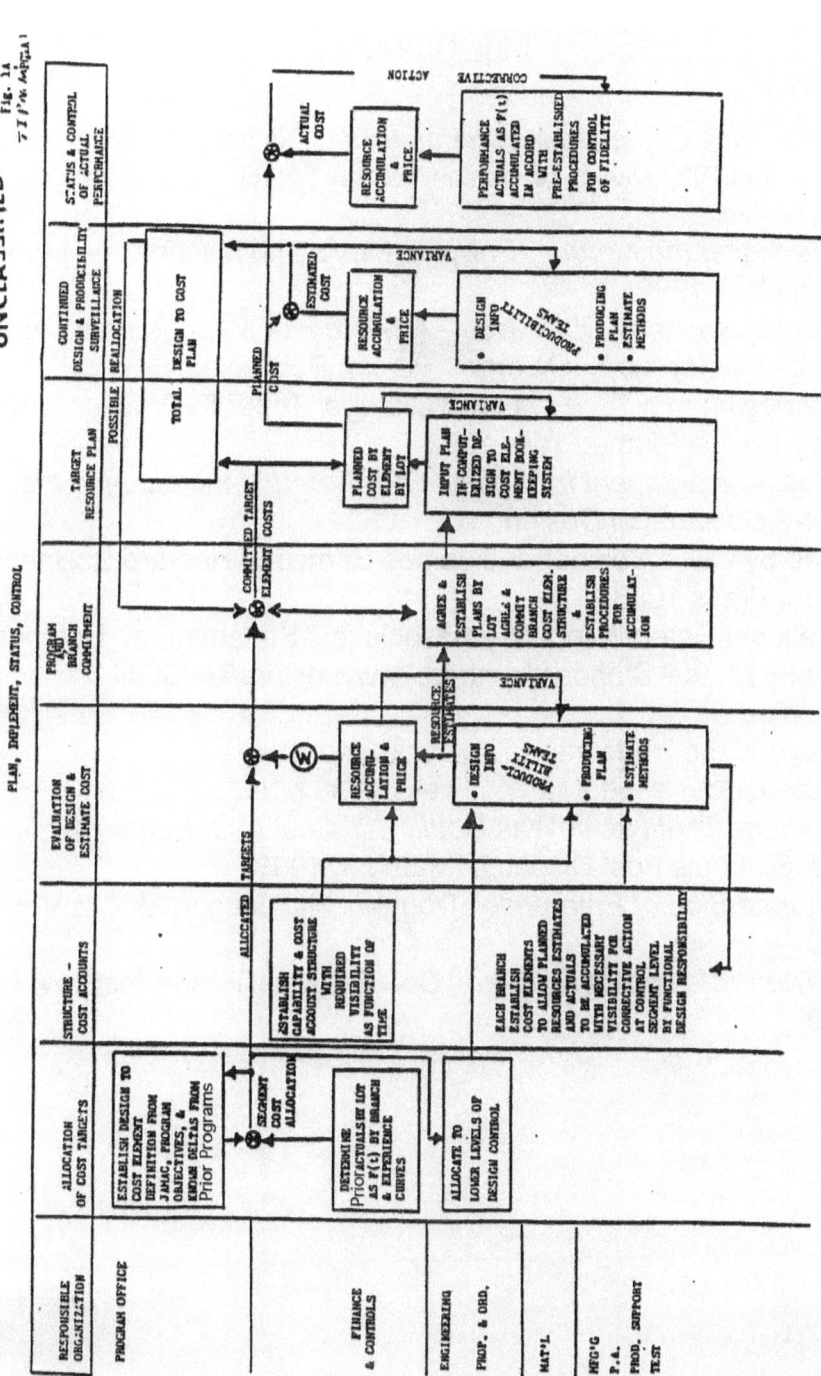

UNCLASSIFIED

THE DESIGN TO COST PROCESS
PLAN, IMPLEMENT, STATUS, CONTROL

BIBLIOGRAPHY

1. *Enhancing Organizational Performance*   National Academy Press Publication,1997 Daniel Druckman, Jerome Singer, and Harold Van Cott, Editors

2. *Managing the Merger*   Philip H. Mirvis and Mitchell Lee Marks. Prentis Hall 1992

3. *Management by Objectives - A System of Management Leadership*   by George S. Odiorne. Pitman Publishing 1965

4. *Managing in a Time of Great Change*   Peter F. Drucker Truly Talley Books/ Plume Press 1998

5. *Cost Management for Today's Advanced Manufacturing the CAM-1 Conceptual Design*
Edited by Callie Berliner and James Brimson. Harvard Business School Press 1988

6. National Defense Industry Association Statement of Defense Industry Ethical Standards. https://www.dii.org/about/dii-principles

7. Beyond the Horizons – The Lockheed Story
Walter J. Boyne   St. Martins Press 1998 p 357

8. *A Plane That Never Was Could Still Cost Us a Bundle* Philip Dine St. Louis Post Dispatch March 8, 1998

9. *Human Side of Enterprise*   Douglas MacGregor; McGraw Hill 1960

10. *The Professional Manager,* Douglas MacGregor; McGraw Hill 1968